COURAGE
TO CHANGE

COURAGE TO CHANGE

Keystone Speakers

Solid Foundations for Success in Business and Life

CORNERSTONES & KEYSTONES SERIES
BOOK 4

Courage to Change

For permission requests, contact the publisher at
keystonespeakers@gmail.com

ISBN: 978-0-9686465-7-1

Publisher: Keystone Speakers
Copyediting: Red Shoes Writing Solutions
Cover design and layout: Impress Printers
Photography: Carey Lauder for Man Doan, Laverne Wojciechowski,
            Greg Wood, Michael Bayer

First Edition, October 2020

Ordering Information: Quantity sales. Special discounts available for bulk purchases. For details, contact the publisher at keystonespeakers@gmail.com

www.keystonespeakers.ca

DEDICATION

This book is dedicated to MyLinh and the Doans, Andrew and Jessamine Gray, Lorise Wojciechowski and Jared Vogt, Samantha Bryden and sons, the late Doris Lewy and Lionel Guerard, Ian R. and Dave P., Barbara Bayer and Dan Deurbrouck, Bill and Bernice Myskiw, and Dorothy Clara (Busick) Lamser.

CONTENTS

INTRODUCTION

In 2017, I was thrilled when Keystone Speakers invited me to be one of their guest speakers. The newly formed group, whose purpose was to develop and support professional speakers utilizing the Toastmasters International club model, had published the first book of its Cornerstones & Keystones series, Solid Foundations for Success in Business and in Life, and was seeking advice on how to write their second book, Expanding Your Potential. From my experience, writing the first book is challenging, yet also new and exciting. Tackling the second book? Daunting, bordering on terrifying. I was only too glad to help.

The following year, I offered to host a day-long writers' retreat for the club as they put to paper the wisdom gleaned from their respective successes in both business and life. This resulted in the series' third book, The Journey Continues. It was such a joy working with this talented group that I joined Keystone Speakers as a full member in 2019, excited to contribute to the book series as an editor and fellow writer.

Keystone Speakers is proud to publish its fourth book, Courage to Change. This book is a celebration of the ways in which we personally have brought forth our own determination and grit in order to move through change to achieve personal growth. As we worked through our earlier drafts of this book, the word that came up repeatedly was choice. Courage to change, we learned, is not a personal quality like eye colour – that is to say, you either have it or not – but a choice.

Everyone has some element of courage. Some people naturally express it on a regular basis because it is one of their top strengths. Being courageous feels natural and energizes them. Most of us, however, only tap into courage when the need arises. But, if Greek philosopher Heraclitus is correct – that change is the only constant in life – then perhaps the need for courage is also a constant.

We hope our stories inspire you. May you embrace all of our courage so you can find yours when faced with the change that presents itself in your life.

Kim Hruba, ACB, CL
Cornerstones & Keystones Editor
Founder & President, Red Shoes Writing Solutions

1 | THE INVISIBLE MAN: WHEN HAPPINESS ISN'T ENOUGH
by Man Doan

Everyone has that one experience that makes them look at life with a new set of eyes. For me, it was on Father's Day, June 21, 2015, when I suffered a heart attack and survived after I had just finished my first 10K race. If you have been following the Cornerstones and Keystones series, I have described in length what happened to me, the recovery, and the journey of rediscovering myself and exploring my own potential. Not everybody needs to have a near death experience to look at life differently. There are hundreds of experiences that have had some sort of impact on our lives. Some are very small while some are much more life altering, making you realize you are stuck in a dead end and need to make a change. In this chapter, I want to take you on a different journey and share with you the career-changing moments in my life. I hope that you will find the inspiration and courage to make a change and will be able to accomplish so much more with your life. It certainly worked for me and has worked for most people who I have had a chance to share my story with or mentor in their career.

THE INVISIBLE MAN

After graduating from university, I was lucky to find a job right away and start my career in the Information Technology industry.

In fact, I got multiple offers and had to pick the one that I thought would give me the most opportunities to learn and grow. I was pretty happy and content with my decision. After a few years, I changed jobs a few times and finally ended up in an organization where most of the people in my circle of family and friends would consider good because the job was stable and came with certain perks and benefits. I thought I was set for life and ready to dedicate my talent and skills to developing applications and systems to help make a difference for the people and the clients we served. I was performing well and was pretty sharp with my technical skills. But there was always something in the back of my mind. I felt like the typical "lone programmer" that spoke my own cryptic programming languages who wasn't really communicating with everyone else. I was glued to my cubicle most of the time. I never really fit in or had the conversational exchanges with my colleagues that I wanted to have. I often went to coffee breaks with them but I mostly listened to the conversations. They always encouraged me and included me in the conversations but, as time went by, they got used to my quiet companionship of smiling and nodding, instead of talking. After a while, I dropped out of the group coffee breaks and spent time on my own.

One Halloween, somebody at the office played a prank and made individualized posters that gave everybody a nickname associated with comic book characters. Mine was "The Invisible Man." Not the usual Superman, Spiderman or Batman, but the Invisible Man. It was all fun and games and I knew my co-worker meant no harm. I didn't think much about it until after a while, when I realized that I did feel invisible in the office. Part of the reason why I was so quiet, I knew, was due to the cultural and language barriers that I had been struggling with ever since I came to Canada as an international student.

But the other reason was simply that communication was not my strongest point. I was terrified of public speaking. In my university years, I did not have a chance to practice my presentation skills much. When entering the real world, I was always stressed out over any presentation that I had to make. I had that fear of speaking in a small team meeting every time, let alone public speaking in front of a big crowd. Roy, one of my colleagues, later on jokingly made a comment about me: "I was working with Man for a number of years but I have never heard him speak once. And it's funny that Man was sitting just two cubicles away from me!" When I thought about those years, Roy probably wasn't joking at all. I was quite shy and quiet back then. I was "The Invisible Man."

THE POSTER

One day when I was coming to work I saw a poster about Toastmasters just outside my office. I didn't know anything about Toastmasters at that time. But one thing struck me in the poster, it said: "Do you get nervous when you have to speak in public? Toastmasters can help!" I thought to myself, "Who wouldn't get nervous?" This seemed a perfect opportunity for me to conquer my fear of public speaking and to improve my communication skills. From that point on, every time I walked into my office, I looked at that poster. I stared at it. I wrote down the phone number. I was planning to call that number and see what Toastmasters was all about. I wondered what kind of meeting it would be. How many people would be there? What would they be talking about? Could I be there just to observe and not speak at all? I had so many questions. I was so curious, but I never called. Perhaps, I was busy with work. Perhaps, life just moved on. Or perhaps there was no immediacy or urgency for me to call. I was still performing well at work. I enjoyed what I was doing. Nobody bothered me. I did not bother anybody. After work, at the end of the day, I came back to my close circle of family and friends. Life was good!

But I always felt that there was something missing. It was the weird feeling you have when you know happiness is not enough. I was missing out on many things because I did not talk to people at work as much as I talked to my close friends. I wasn't really my whole self when I was at work. We all know that the workplace is where we spend a large portion of our time, so it's important to try and be as happy there as you can be. I had a good, stable job up to that point. The people in my workplace were very friendly, supportive, and accommodating. I enjoyed my job but I did not feel fulfilled. The problem was me.

I remember attending a seminar and a keynote speaker talked about the importance of networking and communication. He mentioned a quote: "It's not what you know, it's who you know, and who they know." To some extent, it's true. But to get to know people, you have to communicate. I realized that if I was going to do well with what I wanted to do in my life, I needed to get up in front of people and talk. I had always wanted to move up to a management position in my career. However, at that point, I was still nervous every time I had to provide my update in a team meeting, let alone chair a meeting or give some sort of speech as part of management's role. When I attended a course or workshop, I would get really nervous when the instructor asked us to do a round of introductions or present our points of view.

I realized I had to make a change in my life. I had to break that cultural and communication barrier. I started by calling the number on the Toastmasters poster, two years after I first saw it. It turned out that one of the managers in the office, Brian, was a Toastmaster and attended the meetings every week. Later on at a lunch meeting event, I was sitting next to Brian and I inquired about Toastmasters. He kindly invited me to a meeting at his club, The Forks Toastmasters (Club 7373). I attended the first Toastmasters meeting ever in my life in May 2008 as a guest. I joined Toastmasters and delivered my first ice breaker speech shortly after in June 2008 and the rest is history.

MISTER TOASTMASTER

By joining Toastmasters, participating in club meetings regularly, practicing my speeches with a supportive audience, and working on the educational programs, I experienced a quick positive impact in my life. In just a few short months, people started to see a big difference in me. Remember Roy, the colleague who had never heard Man speak once? Later on, it was me who invited him to a Toastmasters meeting and he also joined our club. We have become good friends and have since shared a lot of personal stories and worked on many speeches together. Nowadays, when he talks about me, he still makes the same comment about me being so quiet, but now he adds: "Man won't shut up now. He can talk and talk and talk, so we have to make sure he stops talking when the red light is on!" I took that as a compliment! Over the years, I warmed up to people at work. I even said hello to strangers walking by. I became more involved with Toastmasters and took on various executive roles for the club. I started planning and promoting our Toastmasters events, open houses, and speech contests. As a result, more and more people from my office, as well as from other floors in the building and workplaces nearby, also joined our Toastmasters club. Every Thursday at noon was so much fun at the office because there would be a big group of us getting ready for another entertaining and educational Toastmasters meeting.

Everybody started to talk about Toastmasters: "Who gave a speech today? What was 'Don the Godfather' up to this week? Did you guys do Improv during Tables Topics again?" It was a real buzz at the office. We all had fun while learning and improving our communication and leadership skills.

After a few years with Toastmasters, I expanded my personal and professional networks. I learned so much, I decided to take on more challenges and became more involved from the club to the district level. I am proud to say that I have held all the executive roles at the club level including President, Vice President of Education, Membership, Public Relations, Treasurer, Secretary, and Sergeant at Arms. At the district level, I served as an Area Governor, Mentor and Club Coach, and other countless roles whenever there was a need or gap that the district needed to fill to help members and clubs in their respective communities. Each opportunity gave me a unique experience that I could learn and apply for myself. It was very rewarding and well worth the time. At a district conference in 2016, I was taken by surprise when I was honoured with the Division Director of the Year award in District 64 representing all of Manitoba, northwestern Ontario, and northwestern Minnesota. But the most rewarding part of all has been the experiences themselves. I have had the opportunity to meet and connect with people of all backgrounds. I have been invited to speak on professional and personal development topics. I have been honoured to share my stories and experiences to help people explore their own potential and achieve success.

THE MOVE

Everyone, including me, hits roadblocks and setbacks, but I have always been able to push through them and stay on track.

For a long time, I was at the top of my game. I enjoyed the professional work I was doing and the challenges that came with it. Since joining Toastmasters, I had been very satisfied with my career progression and fortunate to have moved forward within the organization I was with. I was happy and content with my progress and accomplishments. I also enjoyed the stability and routine. But sometimes, it's easy for us to slip into the stagnant waters of stability, certainty, and comfort. Like putting on weight, it happens gradually, until one day you notice how out of shape you have become. I realized I had to make a change in my career.

When an opportunity came up, luckily, all my personal growth, continuous improvement, lifelong learning investments and Toastmaster efforts paid off. This time, I stepped out of my comfort zone again in a big way. I left the organization that I had been with for most of my career. It was certainly not an easy decision. I had reached the pinnacle of my career and everybody in my family thought I was set for life. I thought I would stay with the same organization until retirement too. But then there was that feeling inside me again. That weird feeling you have when you know happiness is not enough. I was reminded of the 3 Cs of life: choices, chances, changes. "You must make a choice to take a chance or your life will never change." I felt that this particular move would take my life and career exactly where it should be.

BUILD A BETTER YOU

I have been an active member with Toastmasters for over a decade. I wish I would have joined earlier. It would have made my life much easier. But it's better late than never. I came to Toastmasters first to conquer my fear of public speaking. Toastmasters also helped me become a more competent speaker and effective leader. It has helped me grow personally and professionally. But most of all, Toastmasters has given me the confidence I needed to express myself, to realize my full potential, and do so much more with my life. Now, I stay involved with Toastmasters and continue because of the people. I want to give back and help new members explore their potential. I enjoy the personal stories and inspiring speeches that I get to hear from members of all backgrounds, races, cultures, genders, ages, abilities, ideologies, and ways of thinking. I enjoy the thrill of speech contests. I enjoy the camaraderie and companionship of fellow toastmasters at the clubs and district events. Beyond communication and leadership development, Toastmasters certainly feels like a family to me.

We all have goals to better ourselves in different ways. But good intentions often don't become action. Sometimes, we can get too comfortable and become complacent. If you find yourself dissatisfied, take action. If you find that weird feeling inside you, when you know happiness is not enough, make a change. I often share with my fellow Toastmasters that one of the most memorable and meaningful investments in my career has been joining Toastmasters. It has opened many doors of opportunity in my life, personally and professionally. From the Invisible Man, I became known as Mister Toastmaster, Mister Man, or just "The Man." I am no longer invisible.

Check out Toastmasters! It will change your life forever!

ABOUT THE AUTHOR
MAN DOAN

Man Doan has over 20 years of knowledge and experience in Information and Communications Technology.

Man holds an MSc in Information Systems, a BSc in Computer Science, and certificates in Business Analysis, Project Management, Organizational Change Management, and Lean continuous improvement. He has many years of experience at the senior management and leadership positions.

Man is an active member with Toastmasters International. He has served in many leadership positions in District 64 and received numerous awards for communication and leadership excellence. Man won first place three times at the Division level (International Speech and Table Topics contests) and placed among the top 6 finalists at the District 64 Championship.

Man is passionate about public speaking. He speaks on professional and personal development topics to help people explore their potential and achieve success. Man brings with him incredible energy and passion in everything he does.

Contact:
man@mandoan.com
www.ManDoan.com

2 | ADAPTABILITY: *YOUR* CHOICE
by Karen Kaplen

"The only thing that is constant is change."
– Heraclitus, Greek Philosopher

My father, Eric, one of my greatest heroes, passed away suddenly when I was 13 years old. My mother Margaret, a homemaker, took a year to grieve and to decide what to do. As the breadwinner of the family, she knew she had to go back to work to support herself and me. Having been a teacher years before, she realized she would need to upgrade her skills in order to qualify for her First-Class Teaching Certificate in Manitoba. Not having a car, she traveled with a neighbor to a high school in Winnipeg to take French and Biology. Once she graduated, there were few teaching positions available for her in the Stonewall area outside of Winnipeg where we lived, so she went to Split Lake, Manitoba, nearly 900 kilometers north, to teach elementary school. I was fourteen years old and about to start high school.

After discussion with a Mennonite family who lived in our neighbourhood, my mother decided the best option was for me to attend a boarding school, the Mennonite Collegiate Institute (MCI) in Gretna, Manitoba, along Canada's southern border and 140 kilometers south of Stonewall – in total one thousand kilometers away from my mother.

Growing up in Stonewall, I was used to being able to go out on my bike with my dog and ride about the neighbourhood, visiting friends who lived on farms. I wasn't the strongest reader, but my grandmother helped me improve my reading skills by having me read aloud to her and by keeping me supplied with Nancy Drew mystery novels.

I attended a one-room school in the Rural Municipality of Rosser. We only had one teacher for grades one through eight. All the children would play together at recess and lunch hour. We took thermoses of hot chocolate and spaghetti or sandwiches in our lunch boxes and either were driven to school by parents or rode our bikes. Girls wore skirts or jumpers under ski pants. In the spring and fall, we wore slacks or knee-high shorts and played soft ball or soccer outside. One father set up an ice rink in the winter and we were able to skate. We had an annual Christmas concert, a highlight of the year, with Santa at the end. All the parents attended the concert and we would have cookies and hot chocolate before heading home. My mother would make donuts for all the children. For the final school picnic of the year, we had gunny sack races, three-legged races, and played softball against other schools in the Rosser municipality. We ate hot dogs and ice cream, and drank soft drinks. In grade eight we were the oldest students in the school and were somewhat revered by the younger students.

Going into grade nine at a board school would prove to be a year of many changes leading to personal growth for me in which I learned that adaptability was the key for the courage I needed to adjust to all the change in my life.

At MCI, there were separate classrooms for each grade from nine to twelve and as a grade nine student I would be among the youngest in the school. All the students wore uniforms. The girls wore navy blue dresses with white collars and the boys wore sports coats and dress pants. Girls were not allowed to wear makeup or nail polish.

The second language we learned was German making the minimal amount of French I had learned in grammar school useless. Even the hymns in church were in German. Most of my classmates already knew the German language as they spoke German at home and it was their first language. They used more advanced books in language class whereas I was given elementary books to read.

There were 141 students attending classes that year and around 80 students were living in residence. I was thrust into living in a dormitory with a roommate from a different background than what I was used to. My roommate introduced me to Halvah, sesame seeds crushed up with glucose, vegetable oil, and Soapwort extract. The dining hall served blood sausage and boiled potatoes, soups, cheese, eggs, Zwieback, and fruit-filled pastries. It was good food, just different than what I was used to eating. My roommate and I would sometimes purchase a pint of ice cream with bananas from the local grocery store and eat this as a treat in our dormitory.

It was also a lonely time as many of us who were living in residence had to remain in the dormitory for most weekends of the school year. I found that taking pictures of life in our dormitory was a good way for me to pass the time. All students in residence attended church on Sunday. At MCI, I began to understand that being a Christian meant giving one's life over to love God and serve Him. I was not ready for that type of commitment for, on reflection, I thought it would take away from my sense of individualism.

During the second half of the school year, I got to go away for some weekends. Every time I went away, I would take two suitcases with me. There really was no need to cart so much with me but they helped me feel more secure and relieved my anxiety.

I learned a lot about the Mennonite culture and I now feel much richer for this experience. I also learned about adjusting to a new way of life, sharing personal space with a roommate and living in a dormitory, eating different foods, hearing different music, hearing a different language being spoken, and experiencing a different way of being. But I held back in giving my opinion on things. I felt more comfortable observing rather than being outspoken and perhaps revealing my true character. I missed the freedom of being able to catch tadpoles in the spring, ride my bike to friends' homes, and play softball and soccer games at school. I missed my mom's cooking – her homemade meat pies, toad-in-the-holes, creamed corn, beets with white sauce, fresh breads, and custards – and baking cakes, something I could not do at MCI. I missed my freedom. I missed my old life. I missed my mother. I missed my dog. I missed my home.

In grade ten I, was fortunate to be able to move back to Stonewall and board with a retired farmer and his wife who lived only two and a half miles from my old house. I stayed with the Bakers for only a year until my mother found a job teaching mentally challenged people in Stonewall, allowing us to move back into our old home. My mother bought a car and I drove her to school each day and then I drove on to high school. It was good being back in a familiar atmosphere with fellow students I had known most of my life and it was enjoyable making new friends at the nearby high school.

After high school graduation I had the choice of going to college or going on a trip to Sweden. I chose the latter because, in those days, I didn't feel I was smart enough to go to college. When I returned, I was hired as a typist at Standard Aero where I met my future husband. After we got married, we both left Standard Aero and started a family. My husband purchased a sporting goods business and I worked in the family business for many years gaining experience in sales and bookkeeping.

Having worked in the retail service industry for over 15 years, I wanted to change my career path. My children were teenagers by this time and being a parent, I realized I had a lot of transferable skills. I started taking night school courses in programs that were used in office environments then decided to go back to school full time. I took a bookkeeping course at Red River Community College, received a Clerical Bookkeeping Certificate, then started looking for administrative work.

I applied for many jobs but without success in attaining a permanent position. I eventually got hired by a temporary office service company and this gave me experience in working in many office environments from small insurance offices to large corporations. However, nothing was leading to permanent work.

In one position I was hired as a temporary worker in an accounting department. I liked working for the company, but accounting was not my forte. Once, when I was not quick enough in calculating and made a mistake in the procedure, my immediate supervisor reprimanded me severely in front of my colleagues. I had tears in my eyes, but I held them back. Later that week, I was laid off from that position and I gladly moved on.

I have been laid off a few times in my working life. If you are laid off from a job, it's my experience that it is important to remain gracious in your exit. Being bitter and angry is not in anyone's best interests. Negative traits have a way of returning to sender.

When I was laid off from a sales job, I went to the employment office every weekday checking for work. I applied for at least five to seven jobs a week. Finally, the employment office asked if I would like to join a job finders club. I jumped at the chance. This was a two-week program in which I learned to do resume writing and did mock job interviews. I learned that I had been using a totally wrong approach in interviews.

When asked questions by a potential employer, I would talk about my skills and then say something negative about what I didn't do well. As a result, I ended up shooting myself in the foot. The job finders club helped me overcome my negative interview skills and helped me learn how to sell myself to a prospective employer in a positive manner.

When change occurs, all sorts of emotions and questions arise. What can one do? How will a person get past this? Give yourself permission to take some time to evaluate what has happened, brainstorm some possible solutions, and only then can you move on. In the case of a job loss, was this position the "right fit?" Did your qualifications measure up to what your employer's expectations were? Was there a personality conflict with the rest of the staff? Adaptability is key in making change, but sometimes, no matter what you do, it might be best to realize the job was not the right fit and move on.

Eventually, I got a job working as a receptionist in a not-for-profit agency. The people I met liked me and I enjoyed interacting with them. I realized I was much happier working directly with the consumer groups for people living with schizophrenia and helping them learn better coping mechanisms. This was a much better fit for me. My employer and I mutually benefited from the experience and I had found my niche in life at last.

I worked as the secretary for the Manitoba Schizophrenia Society for seven years. I was then offered a position as a group facilitator because of the way I interacted with people who lived with a mental illness. I had no previous experience working with people living with a mental illness, I just treated everyone I met the way I like to be treated, without prejudice or stigma. It never occurred to me that we should treat others any differently than we would like to be treated ourselves.

Leading groups turned out to be a perfect fit for me. I never realized I would be good as a facilitator until a co-worker pointed this out to my supervisor who in turn offered me the position of working as a peer support worker facilitating and organizing group activities, planning programs, and assisting the editor of "The Sensitive Scoop, a newsletter for people living with a mental illness.

It's imperative to find your passion in life and follow it if you can. Adapting to a new role can be a real eye opener as you discover abilities you may never have realized you had.

In order to stay current in the business world, we need to be willing to upgrade our skills. When I began working with groups, I enrolled in night school classes in the Applied Counselling Skills continuing education course at a local college. I surprised myself by being on the Dean's honor list when I graduated. I am continuing to work towards completing the Applied Counselling course at the University of Manitoba with two more courses to complete before I finish the program. Going to school at a later age makes me realize that we are never too old to learn new things. In life we are constantly learning.

I've grown a lot from the somewhat reserved girl I was in my teens at boarding school.

Boarding school taught me that I could adapt to any situation that life hands me whether it be living in a different place, adapting to a different culture, and hearing a different language being spoken.

Job change taught me that you always need to be ready and

open to making changes in life and with that you need to be eager to learn new skills. Every job is different and every company has their own way of doing things. Be able to adapt to that company's way of operating and if you can't, ask yourself whether this job is the right fit for you.

Going to school later in life taught me that we're never too old to learn. As I grow older, I have found that I have a more mature attitude to learning. I am more eager to excel than I was in high school when socializing seemed to be more of priority.

If we learn to adapt to challenging situations and set our minds to do something, we can accomplish almost anything. All these life experiences have helped me to build a strong character. I have the confidence and resilience to never give up. If one comes to an obstacle it is time to pause, think things through, and plan a strategy to move forward.

Be adaptable, be eager to continue learning, and be willing to change. By doing so, you will find the right fit for you and the key to success in business and in life.

ABOUT THE AUTHOR
KAREN KAPLEN

Karen Kaplen is a Peer Support worker with the Manitoba Schizophrenia Society. For over 18 years she has facilitated support groups for people living with a mental illness. She has a unique gift of humility, compassion, and making others feel special. Her core belief is that we should treat all people the way we would like to be treated.

In April 2016, she received the Women Helping Women award from Soroptimist International of Winnipeg and was the keynote speaker at the 2016 Soroptimist of Winnipeg presentation. On February 7, 2020, Karen was honoured as a caregiver of people living with mental illness and was recognized by friends, family, and co-workers at a surprise luncheon hosted by Ify Chiwetelu and Trevor Dineen of CBC Radio's *Now or Never* program.

Karen is available as a keynote speaker and for workshops on topics such as: Supporting People Living with a Mental Illness, The Importance of Using Appropriate Language in Mental Health, and We're All People First.

Contact:
kkaplen@mts.net

3 | LETTING GO OF THE OLD AND BUILDING NEW

by Laverne Wojciechowski

I was doing laundry when, all of a sudden, I heard the washing machine stop mid-cycle. I ran downstairs. The machine was half full of water. I turned the knobs which got it to spin, but it wouldn't wash.

Frustrated, I went upstairs and decided to wash the dirty dishes while I tried to think of what else to try. I turned on the tap in the kitchen sink. To my surprise no water came out. The washing machine wasn't broken – the water pump wasn't working!

Four days before I was leaving on my trip to Lymington, UK, in the middle of a cold winter, and the water pump had died. I couldn't wash the clothes. I couldn't wash the dirty dishes. I couldn't flush the toilet. I couldn't bathe. What was I going to do?

I was preparing for my first overseas trip to the "big show" – the annual conference for pumpkin growers. *So much for washing the clothes I wanted to take on the trip*, I thought, as I pulled the sopping wet garments from the machine and placed them in the laundry basket to take to the kitchen sink for wringing out.

Now, not only did I need to pack for my trip, I needed to figure out how to get the water pump fixed. I called all the local plumbers to see if anyone could fix my pump right away before I left for Lymington, but everyone was either away on winter vacation, recovering from surgery, or not returning my calls. I finally found one from the neighbouring town. When he arrived, I handed him my spare house keys as I rushed out the door and said, "I'm leaving the country. I'll be back in a week. Just fix it."

Have you ever had to make a change? A really big change? A change *so big* that it would change your life forever? That broken water pump set me on a path that would change my life forever at the pumpkin patch.

While I was in Lymington, I saw many old houses. *Lots* of old houses that reminded me of my situation back home. My house was old but not turn-of-the-century old. Nevertheless, I grew up in that house and it was the only house I had ever known. There were so many things that needed fixing. The foundation was cracked and shifting. The plumbing was original and the patches upon patches were leaking. The windows were original and starting to crack. The wooden window frames were starting to rot. I debated: Should I fix the house or build a new one? Do I have the money to fix or to build? I reasoned that, if I fixed the house, I would still have an old house, whereas if I built, I could design a house to fit my needs and it wouldn't need fixing. By the time my trip was over, I'd decided: a new house it was going to be.

When I returned home, I consulted some friends on my new house plan. They all seemed to be in favour of a new build. I didn't want to be in limbo between houses too long or spend a lot of money renting while building, so a ready-to-move home seemed the fastest way to go. The foundation and the house could be built at the same time making it faster to move in than a custom-build house on site.

I realized at this point I was likely going to go through this by myself. I was single, all my immediate family had passed away, and all my relatives lived far away. I didn't want to ask friends for help as that would be a big imposition. Was I up for this? Could I do this on my own? Despite being on my own, I knew I *had* to make a change. I couldn't live anymore with the stress of things breaking down and the cost of fixing them.

What did I want in my new house? What did I like and dislike about the old house? I made a wish list instead of a floor plan. The new house had to have a high vaulted ceiling (for my huge Christmas tree) with tall windows facing the river. It needed an electric fireplace as I didn't want a real fireplace and all the mess it makes. I wanted everything on the main floor, so no basement. I wanted a nice big deck on the front facing the river with flared stairs and no railings blocking my view. I wanted an open space concept so I could exercise, dance, and entertain.

I set up an appointment with a builder and brought my wish list. They said it could be ready in four to five months which meant it would be ready by Christmas. What a present that would be! I was on my way to letting go of the old and bringing in the new.

Once the decision had been made, I would come home every day after work, look in kitchen, and think, *It's not so bad. Why I am doing this again?* Then I would go to the basement and say, "No it's bad, it's bad!" There was a while when, every day, I flopped back and forth: Should I build or should I fix? If I wasn't flip-flopping, I was counting down the days – thirty-fifth last day, thirty-fourth last day, thirty-third last day.

I dragged my feet on packing. This was my childhood home. This was my *life*. In this house, I sang songs with my sister in the living room. We had conversations about our future while washing dishes at the kitchen sink. For birthday parties, my mom gathered all our friends around the table in the tiny kitchen. Now I was moving on to a new life, a new home, but I had no idea what to put in it. Did I want carpet, hardwood or vinyl flooring? What colour did I want the exterior to be? How many rooms did I need? Did I want new furniture? Could I afford the extra cost? As I was packing my personal belongings in the bedroom, I thought, *I've had this furniture all my life. It's time for a change. Let's go new!*

Once the house plans were drawn up, the next trip was to the bank for a mortgage, followed by hiring a lawyer. Then there were the fees, fees, and *more* fees. As the building process progressed, I started bleeding money, $1,000 here and $1,000 there. I wondered when it was going to stop and if I would end up house poor.

The whole process didn't feel real until I saw the orange surveyor crosses and sticks all over the yard. That's when it hit me: I was building a new house! It wasn't the signing of the building contract or the mortgage that made it real – it was those crosses and sticks. I was building a new home and I still had an entire house to empty!

The demolition was scheduled to happen right after the August civic holiday. Some friends came a week or two before "D-day" to help me pack. One day, I had so many helpers, I couldn't concentrate on packing. One person was retrieving copper pipe and anything metal that could be recycled; another was moving heavy items out of the house while the rest were sorting my stuff. They kept asking questions, questions, and *more* questions. *Stop with all the questions,* I thought. When we finally broke for supper, they asked where I wanted to eat. I told them, "You decide. I cannot possibly make another decision today. Just put me in the car, drive me to food, and select my dinner." My head literally hurt with all the decisions I needed to make.

I remember lying on the couch in the rental house, exhausted after a day of packing, listening to all the sounds. I heard the furnace fan go on, the refrigerator hum, the water run in the toilet, the creaky floor boards rebound. Wait a minute, *the water should not be running in the toilet.* Panic stricken, I ran to the bathroom. This wasn't even my house and it had a water problem just like mine did.

I went back to lie down on the couch. Then the panic attack hit. My stomach tightened and my breathing sped up. *What am I doing?* I would be knocking down my own house in a week! I lay there, wishing somebody was there to calm me down. Then I remembered the words from Pam Grout's book, *Thank and Grow Rich:* "It's okay." That's right, it *was* okay. What had changed in the last five minutes? Nothing. Just my thoughts. At that moment I realized it was all good and, after that, I never had another panic attack. Once I set my mind on building the new house, I went full steam ahead, eyes forward, never looking back. My life was never going to be the same again, so I might as well enjoy the ride. *It's okay.*

Finally, the day before the demolition arrived. I was still collecting a few things and had to cut the grass one last time to make the house look good. I know it sounds odd; the grass near the house was all going to be torn up by the demolition equipment, but I had to cut the grass. Maybe I felt my dad's presence and he always liked a well-cut lawn. Maybe I felt it was like a funeral and I was dressing the house nicely for the last time. I rode around on the riding lawn mower admiring the house and it brought back memories of all the good times.

The day of the demolition, I walked through the house one last time, saying goodbye out loud to each room. My voice echoed in the empty house. When I heard the excavator coming up the driveway, I got butterflies in my stomach.

I did one more walk-through of the house with the builder and demo contractor. The demo contractor positioned the excavator and I got to take the first swing at the roof. I had never operated equipment like this before and the controls were surprisingly sensitive. I felt a moment of excitement. I hit the roof with the excavator's bucket and the entire roof shook. The smile on my face that stretched from cheek to cheek said it all as I exited the excavator's cab. I was sad to part with my childhood home, but I was happy because I was SURE I was moving on to bigger and better things.

I watched all day as the house got demolished. It felt weird seeing nothing in its spot after it was all gone, like my life history had been wiped out. The empty yard made me really feel like I had just entered a no man's land between the worlds of old and new.

I visited the site every day and watched the new house being built before my eyes. I felt the excitement of my "new baby" being born. I remember squealing with delight when I saw my towel bars! (Yes, towel bars excited me!) I remember when the lights were installed and I could actually turn them on and not need a flashlight anymore. I remember how the house looked with the outside lights on for the first time. My wish for a dream home was coming true! During the building process, I would go to the house and journal my thoughts. I remember someone telling me how bold it was of me to demolish the old house and build new. *Be bold* were the words stamped on the cover of that year's journal.

The contractors finished the house enough for me to move in by December 23rd and the house was cleaned on December 24th. The pieces were heavy and it was difficult to assemble, but the next day my friend Tatyana and I put up my 12-foot Christmas tree in my new living room overlooking the river. I now had my Christmas house! To this day, Christmas day feels like the house's birthday.

The first night I spent in the house, I slept on an air mattress because my new bed hadn't arrived yet. Every time I moved, the mattress squeaked as it rubbed the floor. I heard and felt every little noise the ductwork made as the metal expanded and contracted. It was a cold winter night and I had forgotten to turn the thermostat up. I was too tired to get up and look how to do it so I just piled on the blankets.

On New Year's Eve, I was officially moved in. I was so exhausted, but I stayed up until midnight to ring in 2017 anyway to celebrate my first New Year's Eve in my new house. Then I crashed and went to bed. New Year's Day, I sat in my recliner and did nothing for the entire day.

Those first few months felt like living in a hotel. In a hotel everything is new to you and you need to figure out how things like the taps and lights work. I had to learn how to operate the new garage door opener, the in-floor heating, the HRV unit, the electric furnace, fridge, microwave, and water treatment system. At a hotel, you need to pack and unpack. At the house, I was still unpacking all my belongings. When I went to the pumpkin conference in Niagara Falls a few months later, it felt like I was going from one hotel – my home – to another. It took a long, long time before the new house felt like home instead of a hotel.

Now I love my new house. It's easy to maintain and I don't worry anymore about things falling apart. Even though it is twice as big, the energy bills are twice as small. I don't have to put plastic sheets on the windows for the winter. No straw bales are needed for the septic field. No snow fence is needed since the house is oriented differently. No heavy air conditioner needs to be installed in the bedroom window. I made the best decision *ever* even though it was a very difficult one to make. Throughout that year, from decision to final product, I grew as a person. I became confident in my ability to change and go through change by myself. I had to be resourceful. I discovered that fond memories are not forgotten. A house does not define you as a person. Most importantly, the confidence in doing this by myself has inspired me and opened me up to new possibilities.

Have the courage to change – to let go of the old to make room for something new – and keep growing!

ABOUT THE AUTHOR
LAVERNE WOJCIECHOWSKI

Laverne is a dynamic, entertaining speaker who will have your audience laughing and inspired to accomplish their goals. Laverne believes in leading by example, becoming the role model for the organization.

Laverne has over 25 years of experience in the scientific field but gardening is one of her favourite hobbies. She has been growing giant pumpkins (some over 500 lbs.!) most of her life. She shares her experiences in the pumpkin patch and how those experiences, applied to your personal life and business, will make your personal life bloom and will make your business flourish and grow. She believes in cultivating the power of positive thinking for personal growth.

Laverne believes communication skills are important in everyday life and it's not just what you say but the visual clues that are important as well.

Contact:
wojciech@mymts.net

4 | SPEECH NINJA
by Stephen Bryden

Panic flashed through my mind as if I were about to be thrown into a volcano. The conference had a packed house from side to side and front to back. The room felt electric and the noise of the excited crowd was intense. Had I actually volunteered to step in front of this *massive* audience to introduce the keynote speaker? I could feel my heart start to pound through my chest.

This small role was a huge step for me. Ten years ago, I could hardly stand in front of a meeting room of ten people without shaking. And now here I was at Vision Quest, a large annual Winnipeg conference that promotes Indigenous economic development and community well-being. I was about to introduce Don Burnstick, a nationally renowned Indigenous comedian and wellness speaker, who was one of the top headliners and a main draw for the conference itself.

Previous to my volunteering at Vision Quest, I knew Don was a super funny comedian but I wasn't fully aware that his keynotes were also about healing Indigenous youth and communities. I discovered his presentations to be motivational and grounded in real-world challenges that he and his community currently face. His keynotes masterfully connect with Indigenous youth helping them navigate the challenges they experience and face every day.

Becoming fully aware of his stature elevated my respect for

him even more, but didn't help with my nervousness. I didn't feel like I belonged there to even introduce him. Deep down, however, my courage told me that this tiny role of mine was an opportunity to challenge myself. Not only would I get to watch and learn from a well-respected leader who effectively communicates valuable messages and transforms minds and communities, it would also be a chance to stretch my speaking skills and test drive my nerves.

I checked my watch. It was almost time to rise up from my seat and walk up on stage and introduce Don. Time slowed as the familiar anxiety and tension I got whenever I spoke publicly welled up inside me. My legs trembled and my arms shook. My body tensed. Doubts ran through my mind. Should I even be here? Was I ready to speak in front of such a large audience?

I remember the first time I felt those same distinct feelings. It had been an ordinary day ten years prior. I was sitting at my desk thinking about visiting a local Toastmasters club within the organization I worked for. I had seen an advertisement on my company's internal website. It read: "Are you looking to improve your public speaking skills? Come visit our open house at lunch!"

A commonly held belief about public speaking is that people fear it more than death itself. That might be a myth, but that day, I felt some truth to it because when I read the advertisement it did spark anxiety in me. Would I need to do a speech? What would I do if they asked me to speak and I wasn't prepared? How badly would I embarrass myself? How badly would everyone laugh?

At that time in my career, I had come to a point where I recognized I needed to work on my communication and leadership skills. I was starting to move into leadership roles where those competencies were more critical for my professional success. I always knew I had knowledge and innovative ideas to share, but my anxiety and lack of confidence always inhibited my ability to clearly express them. Despite my mind running wild with possibilities resulting in disaster, I resolved to take that first baby step and attended my first Toastmasters meeting.

I clearly remember stepping into the club meeting room feeling some trepidation about what I would encounter. I had visions of not belonging or being accepted, or maybe not being good enough to join. At that time, I could hardly string a sentence together for small business presentations. Would I be called on to give a keynote speech for the club? GHAAA!

When I stepped into the club meeting room, everyone was happy I was there and I was accepted with open arms. I felt relieved that I wasn't tied to a stake, forced to deliver a three-hour dissertation on the power of public speaking expected to rival a Tony Robbins seminar like I had originally feared.

I felt glad to be a prospective member to the small, but hopeful, club. I was determined to develop my speaking competency and deep down I knew I had already decided I needed to join before I even arrived. I quickly saw this was a friendly and giving group that I could grow with.

When I submitted my formal application, glimmers of excitement, hope, and relief emerged that surprised me. I had just taken a small step towards empowering the expression of my own voice. That tiny bit of courage started a journey of transformation and growth to possibilities that I thought were impossible.

Peter McWilliams said, "Be willing to be uncomfortable. Be comfortable being uncomfortable. It may get tough, but it's a small price to pay for living a dream." Move just past the safe status quo to the sweet spot that is the area where you feel just a little uncomfortable and uneasy. This is the place where you really need to be in order to ensure ongoing improvement and growth to achieve your goals.

As I took a last glance through Don's bio notes that I was to read in his introduction, it dawned on me that while the anxiety I was feeling was basically the same as what I felt ten years ago, the big difference was my line of growth had moved through a thousand practice steps to where I was at the conference. All those year ago, the prospect of me going on stage in front of five hundred people was not in a dream I ever considered. Yet, here I was, as crazy as it seemed, challenging my anxiety, pushing myself to do something more — to go beyond what I originally thought possible. I could feel my palms get a little clammy.

Don may have sensed some of my nervousness because, shortly before show time while I was flipping through my introduction cards, he made some small talk with me. I asked him if he had any preference on how I should introduce him to the audience outside of the notes I had in my hand. He said he wasn't too worried about his introduction, everyone knew him and, in fact, he didn't want a lengthy introduction anyway. Hearing him say that helped remove the pressure of feeling the need to do things perfectly.

Not needing to be perfect reinforced some lessons I had learned in Toastmasters. The audience can't see any awkwardness that might be churning inside me. They're not going to notice the small mistakes I might think I'm making. Through all my practice with Toastmasters, I learned that the motions of being in front of an audience will always feel magnified. So, every bump, stammer, or awkward pause will feel like an obvious blunder. In reality, the audience will never know the difference with any accidental change in a descriptive word, or slight stammer, or a pause that feels too long.

Attention to detail has always been a strength of mine. I am very good at planning and being aware of risks and constraints towards success. When I began my journey in Toastmasters, I applied that same focus for delivering each speech perfectly. I had to get it "just right." Trying to anticipate all outcomes, I would write out every word and then try to memorize it verbatim. I was always so careful to craft every sentence to the smallest detail.

Eventually a question emerged within me: Was I more worried about making a mistake at the podium or about communicating the message the most effective way possible to the audience? I realized I was more worried about my delivery than I was about connecting with my audience. My attention to detail and over compensation towards perfection quickly became my weakness! I needed to work hard to let go of placing too much focus on preparing for invisible mistakes and instead open myself up to the possibility of them.

Striving for the perfect written word for a speech created two problems. First, the written word sounds different when read aloud than when it is read in the mind. People don't typically converse with perfect grammatical flow in a structurally perfect way. Secondly, over crafting a speech can make it sound too robotic and unnatural creating a cold connection with the audience.

To engage an audience you need to be authentic and show some vulnerability. Small imperfections and speaking to the ear versus the page helps with this. This means speaking as naturally as possible and letting your personality shine through.

To this day, I remind myself that the purpose of any presentation is to engage with the audience and to use every opportunity I can to build rapport with them. The primary goal is to maximize the impact of my message. This in turn maximizes my chance for the message to be received in a meaningful way to inspire the audience to make a decision, to make a change in mindset, or to take a decisive action.

As a challenge, try to observe when people are speaking naturally in day-to-day conversations. Notice how people tend to use simpler words that are strung together organically with their unique personality infused into the conversation rather than a barrage of technically and grammatically perfect language.

It is important to point out that this doesn't mean a speech isn't crafted at all. Instead it is more of a stealthy ninja's plan to be practiced and written to sound like it wasn't! Your speech should come across sounding like it was spoken for the first time off the cuff and not practiced a hundred times before, even though it is.

It was time. I nodded to Don and asked if he was ready. He nodded back. I stood up and walked to the stairs by the stage. My pounding heart became more pronounced in my chest and I could feel my anxiety begin to rise. I thought about Don's introduction in my head and the words on the cards in my hand.

The crowd seemed to quiet just a little as I stepped on to the stage. Though I was nervous, I also felt some excitement come back to me and was grateful for its ability to counter balance my anxiety. Those positive feelings of confidence are also something that had been building inside me over the years. My courage had truly grown and, standing at the podium, I felt I was about to break another barrier in my growth. Alternatively, I could also keel over and explode at the microphone because, you know, public speaking has been known to cause death through spontaneous combustion!

Before I started Toastmasters I had a mindset that I just couldn't do it. I had all the reasons in the world why. I didn't have the experience. I didn't have the knowledge. I wasn't in the right place. I didn't have time. I would make mistakes. I wouldn't be able to deliver. My fears and lack of confidence constantly told me no. Because I had those thoughts, I believed them and so I embodied them.

Sometimes a small baby step of courage is the thing required to spark a change that will lead to true transformation towards your full potential. I took that step ten years ago by joining Toastmasters. Soon after, I began to notice small changes in me. I felt more comfortable speaking in front of small groups. I began going to small conferences by myself and started to volunteer and give back more. I continually achieved small victories in those very places where I thought I couldn't. My confidence continued to grow to accommodate bigger and bigger challenges.

As I crossed the stage, I could feel all eyes on me. When I arrived at the podium I could hear my own breath amplified by the microphone. My clammy left hand holding the intro cards began to shake. If my hand shook any more, I would be able to start a one-handed fire.

I looked across the immense room and saw the entrance door at the back. It looked small, so far in the distance. There was no backing out now. The ceiling felt very high and I felt very, very small. I paused, composed myself, and then greeted the room with a slightly shaky: "Good afternoon and welcome!" The few seconds pause of silence felt like an awkward five minutes for me. I glanced down as I brought my left hand to rest on the podium. I thought to myself, "Nope…no fire… this is good. Fire is bad. I am not spontaneously combusting." With my heart still pounding, I launched into Don's bio and his introduction to the audience.

I can't say that I delivered the best introduction that had ever been done in the history of the convention center. I can say that I didn't stumble on my words so terribly that I couldn't speak at all. I can also say my shaking hand didn't start a fire and didn't impact my delivery. And when I finished the introduction, the audience applauded warmly, acknowledging Don Burnstick to the stage.

After I handed the stage off to Don, I was mesmerized as he delivered his keynote presentation. Just like a master black belt speech ninja, Don delivered amazingly powerful healing messages, skillfully intertwining humour that flowed like he had never said these things before, all infused with his authentic personality and leadership shining through. I felt a chill witnessing how he connected with the audience, helping to transform their mindset right before my eyes. At that point I knew my introduction of Don was a long, long forgotten memory in the audience's mind. At the same time, this opportunity was one of the most memorable for me. I had taken another huge step of growth and it felt awesome.

There is a quote I read recently in which John Maxwell asks a simple question: "When was the last time you did something for the first time?" I think this summarizes my journey with Toastmasters. It all started with being motivated to move past my anxiety and fear to try something new. It changed my mindset and empowered me to grow as a better person, enabling me to discover dreams I never thought were even possible.

ABOUT THE AUTHOR
STEPHEN BRYDEN

Stephen is a proven business and technology leader with over twenty years of experience through industry change. He values lifelong learning and holds a Project Manager Professional (PMP) designation, a Management Certificate, Applied Project Management Certificate, Bachelor's degree in Psychology & Sociology, and a Computer Engineering Diploma.

Stephen addresses a variety of communication and leadership concepts through his keynotes, workshops, and books. He believes effective communication is key for organizations to thrive through change and disruption. He develops and cultivates leaders and organizations to become better communicators, empowering them to positively serve their customers.

He is happily married to his wife, Samantha, and has two boys, Jacob and Alexander. Stephen is a longtime member of Toastmasters International has served in many Toastmasters leadership positions including Secretary, VP Membership, President, Area Director and Division Director.

Contact:
ssbryden@shaw.ca

5 | THE ABCs TO ORGANIZATIONAL CHANGE
by Dorian Guerard

The chapter president stated: "The next order of business is the motion to disband Manitoba P.E.O Chapter AZ."

There was an audible gasp in the room.

Our chapter had spent the past 50 years proudly following the Philanthropic Educational Organization (P.E.O.) vision of assisting qualified women with their educational needs through various loans, awards, grants, and scholarships. We had seen women's lives change with the help of our projects and with the personal support of our members. Many had gone on to use their education to become leaders in fields such as education, science, music, medicine, and even massage therapy.

I credited P.E.O. with changing my life by helping me develop confidence in my own abilities. I joined when my children were small, just to get out of the house, and discovered skills in running meetings, working on committees, and implementing parliamentary procedure. I learned about the important work of philanthropies and discovered there was no end to the life-changing possibilities that emerged when we worked together toward a common goal. The fact there had been discussions about disbanding the chapter was shocking.

Fortunately, the motion to disband was a bylaw change

which required prior notice to the membership, and this had not been done. The motion was ruled out of order. This gave us time to act. Jane, one of our members, stepped up and reminded us how we had helped her – a mother of two small children whose abusive live-in partner was taking drugs and had drained her bank account. With our chapter's support, she found the strength to throw him out, get a restraining order and received an educational grant so she could go back to university. She was now a teacher and loving it. She talked about her struggles and how proud she was to have been supported by our chapter. We had given her confidence. She reminded us that her situation was not unique, but typical of women who found themselves in trouble and were unable to obtain funding through other means.

As we remembered how wonderful we had felt by helping her find a new positive path, the atmosphere started to change. If groups like ours were not around, how would these women get the help they needed? We started to realize the full impact of P.E.O. including the fact that, to date, internationally, more than $345 million had been distributed to over 109,000 women from P.E.O.'s six educational projects since the first project was created in 1907.

A small group of members formed an ad hoc committee determined to find a workable path for the chapter to have a future. We used "The ABCs to Organizational Change" to understand how we had come to this point and to identify the steps we could take toward our future. The ABCs are: Analyze the situation, Build a team, (re)Connect core values, Determine how to implement change, and Establish a path.

ANALYZE THE SITUATION – WHAT FACTORS CONTRIBUTED TO THE MOTION TO DISBAND THE CHAPTER?

P.E.O. receives no government funding and funds raised are from our members. Whereas most other women's organizations focus on reproductive issues, we support educational opportunities for women. We target qualified women who are unable to obtain funding through other means, so the reality is we are small fish in a big pond but with a big purpose.

In 2019, P.E.O. celebrated its sesquicentennial. 150 years ago, a small group of female college students established the second women's sorority in the United States. When you consider that back then so few females attended university, that women did not have the vote, and women's rights had not been recognized – their accomplishment was remarkable. P.E.O. later broke away from the sorority model and became a diverse, community-based organization that serves women worldwide and does not discriminate against any woman based on age, ethnicity, religion or education. This was what we were working to save.

First, we realized there were factors outside our control. Many non-profit and service organizations, such as Kinsmen and Rotary, have found their membership dwindling and are trying to find ways to grow. P.E.O. was in the same boat. Second, in prior years, our Provincial Board had provided general support of our chapter, but there had been no specific strategies to help us build membership. Was this a factor in our dwindling numbers? We had not recruited a new member in five years. Third, we analyzed what had caused our chapter to want to disband.

When the chapter president presented the motion to disband, the executive and the committee chairs had all held the same roles for the past four years which is almost always a sign of trouble.

They got bored and discouraged and no one was having any fun. There were no post-meeting programs to learn new points of view and develop our skills. We became more like a social group and with no action items on the agenda, attendance suffered, fewer guests were invited, and membership fell. Despite these problems, some members still wanted things to "stay the way they were" and were resistant to change because this was our "tradition." One specific cause for concern about whether we could continue now was that there were two events that our chapter was required to host in the coming year – a fall luncheon for 80 people and a spring convention for 150 people. Were we a strong enough group to handle these challenges?

BUILD A TEAM TO DISCUSS THE NEXT STEPS.

The ad hoc committee put the following question to a vote of the full membership:

> – *Do you want Chapter AZ to continue being a positive force in your life while helping women with their educational needs? Yes, or No?*
> – *Are you able and willing to help our chapter have a future? Yes, or No?*

The vote was "yes" to both questions, but by a narrow margin.

There was relief and concern on our members' faces. But we weren't quite ready to celebrate. We now had a mandate to rebuild the chapter and create a new path to follow, but we also knew we had some hard work to do as there were still some members who needed to remember that the value of P.E.O.'s mission was worth working toward. This was our last chance to save the chapter.

After some discussion, we elected a four-person chapter-recovery committee. As two provincial events were coming up in the next year, we paired a chairwoman who had experience coordinating conventions with a co-chair who was creative and energetic. The treasurer was familiar with our system of accounting and our membership chair had creative ideas for finding new members. We agreed that our objective was to determine how to make the chapter be relevant in our members' lives again so that we could start to grow.

(re)CONNECT WITH CORE VALUES – HOW DO WE GET BACK TO BELIEVING IN OUR UNIQUE ORGANIZATION?

Chapter AZ members had lost the feeling of how important our organization was, so we started by identifying all the different reasons women had joined our P.E.O. chapter. These reasons included invitation by someone we admired, an interest in learning meeting procedures, a desire to make new friendships with women who shared similar values, to help people in need, and for our own personal growth.

We distributed a questionnaire to help us find a path to follow that would be of benefit to our members with questions such as:

- *What is your main reason for belonging to P.E.O.?*
- *Which P.E.O. projects do you feel most passionate about?*
- *What would you change to our meeting to make it more appealing to you?*

These questions, along with several others, helped us discover what our members felt was needed to make their chapter meeting responsive to their needs. When we felt we were making a difference in our members' lives, we knew we were on the right path to changing the world, one woman at a time.

I heard a story once about a club whose meetings always started with fresh popcorn. It was part of their tradition and one person was delegated to provide it. The club needed to change locations over the years and even purchase its own popcorn machine. They were known across their district as the "popcorn" club. At one point, the delegated popcorn maker found it difficult to take time from work to make the popcorn and it started to affect her job. She hesitantly approached the club executive with her problem as she had been told that popcorn was a key part of their culture. After she explained her dilemma, the president said, "Oh, good. I was getting tired of the popcorn anyway. When the club first started in the company's board room, one of their products was popcorn and they were happy to provide it for us." All those years of following the "tradition" turned out to be not so important after all and had become, not only irrelevant, but detrimental to the club. We needed to learn the lesson that not all traditions are still relevant but our core values are.

DETERMINE HOW TO IMPLEMENT CHANGES.

The specific actions for the chapter-recovery committee were to elect a new slate of officers, develop a strategy for member recruitment, arrange for interesting guest speakers and fun activities, focus on implementing the suggestions from our members, and to celebrate our recipients' achievements. We were optimistic these changes would not only invigorate our current members but make it easier to recruit new ones.

The provincial executive provided additional membership growth ideas such as creating a one-day event designed to introduce guests to the organization. They showed us how to make our meetings more efficient and shared how to find even more information from the P.E.O. Head Office through their new updated website. They reminded us that we constantly need to make changes in our chapter in order to not only survive but thrive.

ESTABLISH A PATH TO FOLLOW FOR THE NEXT YEAR, KEEPING IN MIND ANY UPCOMING EVENTS.

Now that we had a path to follow, it was time to put it into action. We elected a new executive and selected committee chairs that would work toward the chapters' new goals.

Next, the yearbook committee was instructed to schedule meetings for the next year to include programs that followed the members' suggestions for high quality meetings as identified in the questionnaire we had distributed under the (re)Connect with Core Values step. We also challenged each member to be responsible for at least one after-meeting presentation of their choice.

Now that we had an action plan, we met with the provincial executive. They told us we would get a club mentor and help with the 2020 convention. We were delighted to hear that the convention hotel had already been selected.

We had a plan, we had support, and we had a team that was willing to work for a better future. We decided to take one step at a time and follow our plan toward our vision.

THE RESULTS

As an update on our chapter, we held club elections and gave the officers specific roles to follow. Our business meeting was shortened by empowering committees to bring suggestions for the group to vote on and we shared correspondence with all members electronically so highlights brought up at the meeting would go into the minutes. We now had time to enjoy wonderful post-meeting presentations. We learned about "Sarah's Art" – beautiful, hand-painted cards and pictures by one of our member's daughters. We invited a chiropractor who explained the value of regular chiropractic adjustments and we were treated to an interactive presentation by a Program for Continuing Education recipient. We were challenged to identify some of Manitoba's special features such as which Manitoba town "features a 15-foot statue of a mosquito?" (Answer: Komarno) and "has a million-dollar bed and breakfast?" (Answer: Morden) We showed our support to our project recipients and their families at a fun Christmas dinner. Feedback from these actions has been positive and has helped our members look forward to our meetings.

We have made as many changes as possible under our chapter's current bylaws. In our search for the reasons why our chapter was on the brink of disbanding, we discovered a few ideas that we felt could be implemented to make our whole organization even more relevant in today's world. Enabling online meetings, developing a campus club, and changing the name of the greater organization from "P.E.O. Sisterhood," which dates back to our sorority days, to one more inclusive such as "P.E.O. International" are three changes we would like to put forward in the future.

We hosted a successful one-day luncheon for 80 people as practice for the upcoming convention. The assignment of roles, the clear explanation of what was needed, unique presentations, and the team working together, proved to our members that success was possible. We are now working on the upcoming spring convention with excitement, confidence, and a sense of power in our own abilities.

The fact that our chapter wanted to disband is not a unique situation in today's world. Many service clubs and other volunteer organizations have been struggling with membership. Kin Canada, a subsidiary of Kinsmen International, saw membership drop from 25,000 at its peak to less than 6,500 at present. It seems that demands on people's time affect the commitment they are willing to give to these organizations. This creates a loss to both the organization, its members, and especially the programs and benefits for the people they are involved with.

Some groups have opened their meetings to online membership using programs such as GoToMeeting, Skype, and Zoom. This enables members to attend in person and online so people can attend from anywhere in the world if they move away, go on vacation, or are housebound members who still want to attend a meeting. Other groups have started campus clubs to attract younger members and are making meetings more informal and fun, while still aiming to be efficient and productive. They have found that membership can be retained and even enhanced by these methods. These are wonderful suggestions for us to try.

What about you? Is your favourite organization on the path to success or have you lost your way? It is never too soon to review the health of your group using the ABCs to Organizational Change. Analyze the factors that identify if your group is thriving or merely surviving. Build a team of members wanting to improve. (re)Connect Core Values with your members to ensure their needs are being met. Determine what changes are needed so that your future is a positive one. And, last but not least, establish a path to follow to make it happen. These actions will lead your organization to become active, increase membership, and have productive meetings, while ensuring you are not just relying on popcorn.

ABOUT THE AUTHOR
DORIAN GUERARD

Dorian Guerard, DTM, is a speaker and author who brings a diverse set of skills to everything she does. Her leadership experience includes being Provincial President of the P.E.O. Sisterhood. For the term 2014-2015, she was elected Toastmasters International District 64 District Governor. She was proud to lead the team to Distinguished District status and was inducted into the Toastmasters Hall of Fame.

Recent experiences with volunteer organizations that were struggling to survive led her to the *ABCs of Organizational Change*. This provides a workable path to follow so people will feel confident that no stone is left unturned as they come to a decision about the future of their organization. Just like teams often need to make changes to work more effectively, so do organizations, especially if they want to thrive.

Her latest activity is her *Never Too Old or Too Late* blog designed to provide information especially for seniors about travel, cruises, and amazing local finds she calls "Manitoba Treasures."

Contact:
dorian@nevertoooldortoolate.com
(204) 487-0455
www.NeverTooOldOrTooLate.com

6 | BUTTERFLY WINGS: SMALL THINGS CHANGING YOUR WORLD OVER TIME

by Greg Wood

God, grant me the serenity to accept the things I cannot change,
Courage to change the things I can,
And wisdom to know the difference.
– Serenity Prayer by Reinhold Niebuhr

When the Butterfly Effect was first presented as a theory in 1963, its creator Edward Lorenz was mocked by the New York Academy of Sciences. For almost 30 years he remained the object of ridicule and his theory an interesting myth. His theory was that a butterfly flapping its wings in South America could affect weather patterns halfway around the world. The wings would move molecules of air which would move other molecules of air and these would then move other molecules of air and eventually cause the formation of a tornado in the middle of North America. However, in the early 1990s, his theory was proven by a number of physicists. The butterfly effect was accurate. It has since been accorded the status of a law and is now known in scientific circles as "the technical notion of sensitive dependence on initial conditions." This law works on molecules and it works every time. It also works at the human level proving that small changes over time can make a huge difference.

The first time I remember hearing the Serenity Prayer it was August 22, 1980, I was 22 years old, and I was at my very first Alcoholics Anonymous meeting. I needed to quit drinking. I would go out with no intention of drinking and four hours later I would be drunk, banging my head on the bar wondering, "How did this happen AGAIN?" It was time to make a change.

We all sat around on sofas and chairs around the room like we were about to watch the Super Bowl. It seemed like everyone had a cup of coffee and almost everyone was smoking, including me. I had no idea what to expect from the meeting and yet none of it surprised me.

It was a big decision and a huge goal to quit drinking for the rest of my life. Sitting around that room that first night, I learned that the attitude to take was not to quit forever. It wasn't to quit for a year or even for a month. The way to stay sober, I was told, was to quit for 24 hours at a time.

As a former land surveyor, I knew that a difference of one degree in an angle makes a difference of over 90 feet in a mile. A one-degree difference in trajectory over the distance to the moon meant a change of destination of over 6,700 kilometers (4,000 miles). Breaking the goal of becoming sober down into one day at a time would make the change far more palpable. I could do almost anything for one day. If I could change my trajectory by as little as one degree, I would be able to change my course from a downward spiral into more and more drinking to one where I had a family, a job, and a purpose.

FINDING THE WHY

Ralph Waldo Emerson said, "For everything you gain, you lose something." If he is right, then the corollary is also true: for everything you give up, you gain something.

Back when I first decided to quit drinking, all I could think about was that giving up alcohol meant giving up my friends and social life because they revolved around bars and parties. I would no longer be able to hide my horrible dancing skills and social awkwardness behind alcohol. I'd stand out as a not cool dude. I didn't want to lose my friends or be weird, but I knew I needed the change. My friends weren't interested in changing. Only I was. Instead of focusing on what I would be losing, I needed to focus on what I would be gaining. I needed to find the reason – my why – to keep my trajectory moving toward a long and happy life.

My first "why" was easy. I'd met a girl. I was madly in love. She was beautiful, funny, and she loved me too. When I was drunk, I forgot all that. I could see that if I didn't change I would lose the woman I loved. By quitting drinking, I was gaining a relationship that would end up lasting over 40 years.

I tried many times to cut back, to have just one or two drinks, but it just wasn't possible. I could see the downward spiral I was heading for. I knew the next step would be coming in late for work and then skipping work because I was too hungover.

If I chose to stay sober, I would also gain the ability to drive home safely after a night out. I knew I couldn't change my friends' drinking habits, but as the sober one in the group I would be able to get them home safely. My friend's wives would be much happier knowing I would be the one getting everyone home safe. Helping my friends stay safe gave me a sense of purpose.

Finally, by choosing sobriety, I was gaining a healthier lifestyle. I could only imagine what condition my body would be in if I kept drinking What sounded more appealing: to die of old age or cirrhosis of the liver?

It's normal for people facing change to initially focus on what they have to give up. However, anyone leading change needs to focus instead on what will be gained.

What is your why? List all the reasons you can think of for why this change will be good. How will it benefit you? Your family? Your job? Your finances? Your health? Have several "whys" because it is very rare that only one reason will be enough to keep you going. People will fail to do the hard work to make change happen if they don't have enough valid reasons for it. Powerful "whys" will keep you grounded when you hit the messy middle and things get hard. And it *always* gets hard.

YOU ONLY NEED TO TAKE THE NEXT STEP

Motivational speaker and author Jim Rohn said, "Success is nothing more than a few simple disciplines, practiced every day."

When I first realized I needed to make a change, I wasn't sure how to begin. I knew someone who had made the same change and *had* quit drinking, so I reached out to him for help. How had he done it? How had he stayed sober for the last several years? He told me that a life change of this size was too big if you considered quitting forever. He told me that I only had to quit for today. There was nothing I could do about tomorrow so forget about it and concentrate on today.

My friend helped me take the next step. He located a meeting of Alcoholics Anonymous near my home and arranged to pick me up and took me to that first meeting. I attended the meetings three times a week at first to get the support I needed. I learned that the first step in Alcoholics Anonymous was admitting I was powerless over alcohol—that my life had become unmanageable. And if I was powerless then I needed outside help.

You do not need to know every step you will take. You only

need to know what you need to do today. In any change simply ask yourself, "What needs to be done now?"

FIND YOUR PEOPLE

Whenever you make a change, you don't need to do it alone. There are always people who can help. They may be those closest to you, like a spouse. They may be an old friend with life experience that you need. Or it may be a brand new person. It doesn't matter if the change you are making is as personal as sobering up, a change in employment, or a whole new way of doing business. You need a team by your side to help.

Of course my wife was the first one on my list of helpers. She was more than willing to be on my team. That first friend I initially reached out to who had made this change in his own life was also part of my team. He helped me over the years by being someone I could bounce ideas off of. After attending AA meetings for a little while, and on the advice of my friend, I found myself a sponsor. Unlike clubs where you need a sponsor to get in, AA suggests a sponsor so that you can succeed. My sponsor was a man who was a couple of years older than me. I spent many late-night hours drinking coffee with him discussing life and its difficulties as well as the things that were working for me.

Who can help you with the change you are contemplating? Are they family? Friends? Advisors? Venture capitalists? Perhaps they are someone who has made this change themselves. Make yourself a list and ask for their assistance.

EXPECT THE WORST FIRST

There is always a price for change. There will be problems in any change you attempt to make. Pretending there won't be is foolish. But if you expect the worst you can prepare for it.

In the very beginning, I tried to visualize my life without alcohol. Because it was such a large part of my life, I found this quite hard. There were many times when I thought of chucking it all and just going out for a drink again. Following the "do it one day at a time" wisdom, I called my sponsor instead. As I spent those nights at the coffee shop asking him what it was like now that he had been sober for a few years. Was it worth it all?

In response, he asked me a simple question. "Greg, what's the worst thing that could happen if you stuck with the program?" Well, I could lose my friends. I could be bored by not going out several nights a week. I could become a bore myself. Or, I could end up being overcome by temptation and have a drink, which, more often than not, would lead to getting drunk.

He was quick to share his journey with me. Yes, he had lost some friends but he said that was the price I must be willing to pay. If change doesn't cost you anything, there will be no real change. His true friends stayed with him because they wanted the best for him. Now he had a new set of friends who encouraged him and helped him in the rough spots. He also told me that if I *did* get drunk that night, I could wake up the next day and start over again by staying sober for one day at a time.

Spend some time thinking about all the possible problems you will encounter as you make your change and list them out. Get your people to help you prepare.

REVIEW YOUR PROGRESS REGULARLY AND CELEBRATE SUCCESSES

I wonder if Ian MacGregor, former AMAX Corporation board chairman, was thinking of a program like AA when he said, "I work on the same principle as people who train horses. You start with low fences, easily achieved goals, and work up."

It is always important to celebrate successes in any change. In many AA groups, members receive a "chip" or token to celebrate 30 days of sobriety. This is done for two reasons, first to celebrate taking thirty "24 hours at a time" and putting them together. The second reason is because the chip serves as a reminder that the change is still going on one day at a time.

Because doing one day at a time was an easy enough idea to grasp and was something that I could accomplish, I was then able to grow a little bit at a time through the rest of the program. As I write this, I have well over 14,000 days of sobriety. To be clear, it was not always easy, but by not drinking for "just one day" often enough, it became much easier. I still have my 1-year and 5-year tokens. Just like buying a souvenir while on vacation, the chips remind me of where I have been. When I feel those chips in my pocket they remind me of what I have accomplished and how far I've come through small changes. They also remind me to keep going.

In order to celebrate successes, we must first notice them. Then we should share them. Take in a movie, go on a date night to that place you love, sleep in on Saturday. The important thing is to do *something* to reward yourself.

USING THE LESSONS LEARNED

To ease the difficulty that comes with any change, I've gone on to use the invaluable lessons I learned in AA to make other major changes in my life and in my business.

I find my why. Whether it is changing cities or switching careers, finding all of my reasons has been an important part of that change.

I determine what I need to do now. To get in shape it may be to take the stairs or park the car further away from the store. To lose weight, it might be visit a dietician. To change or advance careers, it might mean going back to school.

After all these years I already have my people, but I still need to inform them of the change I am planning.

And I expect and plan for problems. I agree with the philosopher Seneca from 2000 years ago who thought that the best way to remain calm and to be happier was to become a pessimist. Our happiness does not depend so much on what happens to us but to what happens to our expectations. So if I expect many problems and there are only a few, I am happier.

Finally, I review my progress and celebrate successes. I don't wait until I have completed my goal. I celebrate along the way. For example, when I lose a few pounds, I can celebrate by starting with dessert. That may sound counterintuitive to weight loss but celebrating successes like this can make all the difference. I take my diet one day at a time or one pound at a time. And that just gives me more to celebrate.

Every small change we make affects what happens in our lives. There is no magic formula. But by changing the things we can by a small amount, even if it's something as small as the single flap of a butterfly wing or a shift in your trajectory by one degree – over time it all adds up to a huge difference. Change is possible. You only need to take it one day at a time.

ABOUT THE AUTHOR
GREG WOOD

Greg Wood works with organizations that want to *Magically* grow their Leadership so they can: *Levitate* their effectiveness, make problems *Vanish,* and watch profits *Appear!*

Greg has been speaking professionally for over 25 years and has presented in 10 countries on 5 continents. He is a Certified Coach and helps his clients in connecting, to increase their influence and grow their businesses.

After 20 years of running his own business, Greg wanted to move from success to significance. He worked with Leader Impact Group and became a Certified Speaker with the John Maxwell Team.

He recently earned the prestigious Accredited Speaker designation recognizing excellence in professional-level speaking skills and subject matter expertise awarded by Toastmasters International.

Contact:
The Magic of Leadership
greg@gregwood.ca
(204) 779-8066
www.GregWood.ca

7 SPARKLES AND ME
by Michael Bayer

"You're really good with kids. Have you ever thought about becoming a clown?" That was the question that changed my life in ways I could've never imagined.

It was a Saturday afternoon in December and I was making balloon animals for kids at a children's Christmas party where my wife works. For Father's Day several years before, my daughters had given me a bag of balloons, a pump, and a book of instructions on how to make balloon animals. I learned to make balloon animals for them, their friends, kids in the neighborhood, and as Halloween treats for everyone who came to our front door. For the children's Christmas party, my wife had hired a clown who called himself Uncle Dan. He explained that he could do a magic show filled with music and sing-along fun and at the end he would make balloon animals for all the kids. She said no, I have someone who does that. "Perfect," he said. "I'll just run my show a little bit longer and include a few more songs."

I watched his show enthralled. He had the kids singing, laughing, clapping and mesmerized by his magic. After his show, the kids gathered around me. While I made balloon animal after balloon animal, I noticed him glancing over as he packed up his show, watching me interact and joke with the kids. It made me a little nervous. Was I doing everything OK?

Just as Uncle Dan was leaving, he came over to me and asked me the question that would change my life. "Have you ever thought about becoming a clown?" He explained that he belonged to a clown alley and invited me to come to one of their meetings.

We all have seminal moments in our lives. These events can be so impactful that we remember the when and the where and the exact moment that led to those events that would change the very course of our lives. I remember my moment vividly; Uncle Dan standing in front of me, resplendent in his costume, me, frozen in place, holding a half finished balloon in my hands, not knowing how to answer him, and the kids all staring at the two of us.

I thought about Uncle Dan's invitation for several weeks. What would people think of me if I became a clown? I had a responsible job in government. I was well-known professionally in the telecommunications world both in Canada and the United States. I was a dad with two kids. I was a university graduate. Nevertheless, my wife and daughters were hugely supportive and encouraged me to go to the clown alley meeting to learn more. My mother, on the other hand, was horrified that I would even *think* about doing something as stupid as becoming a clown.

With great trepidation I finally decided to attend the meeting. When I called Dan to get the address, he said he would also be at the meeting and was delighted that I was planning to attend.

As I got ready to go, I wondered, What do you wear to a clown alley meeting? Would everyone be in costume? What did Uncle Dan look like under all that makeup, wig, and red nose? Would I recognize him? I decided to dress in regular street clothes and went to the meeting.

There were about twenty people in the room, thankfully, all dressed in normal street clothes. A guy I had never seen in my life came over and warmly greeted me. As soon as he spoke, I recognized his voice. He was Uncle Dan! Everybody was very friendly and offered to teach me clowning skills, help me create a unique clown face. and choose a costume. That night I made the decision that changed my life forever. I joined the clown alley.

I would come to realize many years later that the decision to join the clown alley was the first step into an inter-dimensional wormhole to worlds in a universe that I never knew existed.

First, I had to have a name. I chose Sparkles because of my bright, outgoing personality. Because I was entering this new world with rudimentary balloon sculpting skills, my fellow clowns started there, teaching me how to make more complex animals and shapes like a Harley Davidson motorcycle. Next, they helped me design a face. Every clown has to have a unique face. I had no idea there were so many possibilities. I chose to become a happy, white-faced clown and they taught me how to apply my makeup. Finally, they helped me create a costume. Because of my name, I chose a red wig, topped by a red, sequinned hat, paired with a matching sequinned jacket and fire engine-red pants. A few months after joining, Sparkles the Clown was born and the two of us never looked back.

Now Sparkles and I needed an act. But I had a problem. I couldn't do the typical things clowns do. I couldn't sing, I couldn't dance, and I was a lousy face painter. I had met Lawrence, one of the other members of the club, at the Winnipeg Juggling Festival. Lawrence suggested I include juggling in my clowning repertoire and invited me to the juggling club.

At the juggling club, I stepped into another world in this new parallel universe. After a Sunday morning of throwing balls around, I joined and soon got both of my daughters involved. Together, we learned how to juggle balls, clubs, and devil sticks. I wasn't a very good juggler but we kept going to juggling club because, like the clown alley, it was another fun group of people.

The other members of the juggling club were experienced, polished, professional entertainers. It felt like it would take almost a lifetime of practice to reach their level of excellence. I didn't know if I could develop a profitable clown act based solely on my juggling skills. But I wanted to be a clown that did more than balloon animals. Lawrence suggested that maybe, *just maybe*, I could develop a magic act. I knew nothing of magic. I knew no magic tricks. I had no idea how to structure an act, but I was willing to learn.

I joined the magic club, the *third* world in that parallel universe. The members were all very welcoming. The tricks they performed at the meeting were stunning. Coins vanished and reappeared, silks magically joined, cards mysteriously vanished then appeared on the ceiling. The best part of all, *they taught each other how to do the tricks.* There was only one rule: Never reveal the secret to outsiders. I studied and practiced the tricks, the club members helped me with my performance, and magically, the Sparkles the Clown Magic Show began to appear.

It didn't take long for Sparkles the Clown to become a well-known and very popular local entertainer. I performed Christmas shows, Hanukkah shows, Ramadan celebrations, Baha'i celebrations, Hindu weddings, and countless birthday parties. I busked at farmers markets and appeared in parades and festivals. I loved performing and my full calendar was the sign of Sparkles' success.

I was now living in two separate universes: one as a telecommunications professional and the other as Sparkles the Clown, children's entertainer extraordinaire.

During this time, my wife had joined Toastmasters International to develop public speaking skills for her job. She came home one day very excited about an upcoming conference and wanted me to attend. Unfortunately, I was fully booked with shows. I did agree, however, to attend the Saturday night banquet and speech contest. I sat there mesmerized, listening to six polished speakers deliver their messages each with passion and humor. I leaned over to Lionel, the gentleman sitting beside me, and asked him how I could get on that stage. He replied, "Just sign this membership application and write me a check. We'll teach you the rest."

Little did I know, I was about to enter a fourth world I had no idea had ever existed. I got very involved in the Toastmasters program. I completed the assignments. I spoke as often as I could. Because of my experience as Sparkles, I had no fear of speaking in front of an audience, however, I was still basically an entertainer because the type of shows I did were hugely dependent on constant interaction with an audience. Bev, one of my Toastmasters evaluators, told me I was one of the few people who had to have their enthusiasm restrained. Toastmasters taught me how to write a speech and how to make my presentations sound more natural. I learned structure, flow, and, perhaps, most importantly, how to properly deliver a speech as a speaker instead of as an entertainer. I had great success with Toastmasters and, in 1998, reached the finals of the World Championship of Public Speaking.

Life is always full of strange and unexpected surprises. Some of the surprises are moments of great joy. And some of these surprises can shatter your world – like the Tuesday morning, many years ago, when I was invited to a morning coffee party at which my employer announced the company would be closing its doors in one year and that my 125 colleagues and I would all be laid off.

At the time, this didn't seem like it was going to be the best day of my life. What was I to do? I was in my mid-forties. I had a young family, mortgage, and other responsibilities. This was not the best time to start looking for a job or start over with a new career. I had thought of clowning full time, but the reality of the business was that it was only a part-time, weekend business. I had already cornered that market. Most of my gigs were on the weekends with an occasional kid's party on a weekday. What I needed was a full time job. For six months, I debated what to do before I found another job in my field. I was once again gainfully employed; however, I was very unhappy.

One night over dinner, my wife described a workshop she'd attended that day. She really enjoyed the content and the facilitator's friendly, humorous style. She said, "All day, I was imagining you standing there at the front of the room, delivering this workshop. I think this is something you should try." This sent me down yet *another* wormhole, the world of professional speaking.

This time, I went to a chapter meeting of a professional speaking organization. Despite all my experience as an entertainer and despite all my five years of Toastmasters experience, I felt very overwhelmed and out of place. The members were all highly skilled and polished speakers who were world-class experts in their field. I really didn't think that I would ever reach their level of expertise and speaking excellence. However, with mentors, I worked to select my topics and create my programs. The experience I had gained, not only in Toastmasters and performing, but also in marketing and learning how to create a successful business, held me in good stead. Over the last 23 years, my professional speaking business in healthcare has grown along with my expertise in the industry and I've never looked back or had any regrets.

I realize now that the experiences in each of those different worlds from my alternate universe – clowning, juggling, magic, Toastmasters, and professional speaking – came together to give me the skills and confidence resulting in a successful career that I would never have envisioned that Tuesday morning those many years ago.

All of this happened because I said yes to two questions: "Have you ever thought of becoming a clown?" and "Have you ever thought of becoming a speaker?"

My success was a result of jumping through those wormholes and coming out a highly trained, sought after professional. My willingness to change paths and explore new and exciting possibilities gave me opportunities I would have never dreamed of on my own. Who knows what would've happened to me if I had said no to Uncle Dan. Who knows what would have happened if I hadn't entered the world of magic. Who knows what would've happened if I hadn't joined Toastmasters. Who knows what would've happened, if my wife Barb hadn't made that comment over dinner and if I hadn't entered the world of professional speaking?

What I've learned is that when you come to that seminal moment when you have to make a decision that could change the very direction of your life, you have to have the courage and confidence in yourself to say yes, even if that means going in a direction, and to a place, you could have never imagined.

When you're comfortable where you are, life is easy; you don't want to take risks because the familiar path is safe. The problem is you will never know what you missed. You will never know the opportunities you could have had and the success you would have experienced.

My first seminal moment was in a space of comfort and security. When I said yes to Uncle Dan's question, I didn't need the business of Sparkles; there was no risk. It was very easy to say yes. I did it because it seemed like fun. Not only was it fun, it taught me lessons and helped me develop skills that I would use later to become successful in a field I had never seen myself pursuing.

My second seminal moment came at a time in my life in which I also had comfort and security, but I was very unhappy professionally. When I said yes to becoming a professional speaker and starting my own business, I was instantly transported to a world of great uncertainty and total lack of security. The lessons I learned, because I had the courage to slip into that wormhole gave me the skills and self-confidence to face that new uncertain world and transformed it into one of professional success and accomplishment.

My challenge to you is quite simple. When you come to those seminal moments in your life, think about the possibilities and the new opportunities you will have. Savor the moment and say yes. You never know what opportunities slipping down that wormhole – to a new world in a new universe – will bring you. If you don't, you'll never know what you missed.

ABOUT THE AUTHOR
MICHAEL BAYER

As President of The LEAN Consulting Group, Michael Bayer leads a group of consultants skilled at implementing sustainable LEAN practices. He has an MBA and is a certified LEAN Black Belt for Healthcare. He has his Certified Speaking Professional designation from the National Speakers Association. He is one of 87 who have ever received the Toastmasters Accredited Speaker designation. Michael is one of only six speakers worldwide to hold both designations.

His 12-year background as a senior telecommunications manager in government, coupled with over 22 years at the forefront of initiatives in quality management at hospitals and healthcare organizations across the United States and Canada, have solidified his reputation as a change agent.

Michael teaches organizations the living, breathing, essential LEAN processes that build successful, self-sustaining, profitable corporate cultures.

Contact:
michael@theleanconsultinggroup.com
Phone: (204) 237-9257
Cell: (501) 762-2462
Toll Free: (888) 551-5592
www.TheLeanConsultingGroup.com

8 | MOVING FROM ME TO WE
by Susan Kuz

Growing up I was a very independent type. Just like my dad. We lived in a rural area outside of Winnipeg on a small 5-acre hobby farm on a quiet country road. My parents both grew up *on the farm* and were very resourceful and skilled. If it needed to be done, they could do it themselves. My dad could fix anything and had a huge shop in his garage full of all kinds of spare parts. Just in case something broke – you never knew. The only time we hired someone was for the rare car problem that my dad couldn't fix, or the usual dental and doctor visits. Thank goodness they left that to the professionals.

I'd always thought it a good thing to be so self-reliant and I prided myself in being able to do things on my own. In fact, I'd say I developed a bit of an attitude about this and a preference for autonomy and going it alone. If it needed to be done I could learn how. Before the days of Google or YouTube videos, I relied on a stack of books from the library, a set of instructions, or trial and error as my training ground. I was skilled at teaching myself.

Being independent and skilled at learning new things meant I felt in control. If challenges came my way, for the most part, I felt confident that I could figure things out. After all, working alone has its benefits. You can move swiftly when necessary with no one to slow you down. You can choose your preferred path to the solution. Your meetings are shorter and you get first choice of the donuts.

I also had high expectations of myself and others and was often impatient. In some cases, these personal qualities were assets.

For example, one time I noticed a department at my work was experiencing extensive overtime. Everyone was being asked to work evenings and weekends to catch up but the exponential business growth happening at the same time meant they were falling further and further behind, negating any progress they were making. Stress was mounting, everyone was wilting, and tempers were getting short.

My job had a dotted line connection to the department. My cubicle was in the department but I did a very different job so the overtime didn't directly affect me. I could see, however, that the situation was taking its toll on everyone around me, so I decided to see if I could help.

I interviewed key members of the department to find out more about their processes and workflow. I soon came to realize that the root cause of the backlog was not so much a lack of bodies but more an issue of organization, one that could be helped by an improvement in workflow. Although programming was not my strong suit, I had some experience in a previous role. Truth be known, I programmed simple insurance rate calculators but that was close enough in my book. What I didn't know I could learn.

On my own time I tinkered with database software and figured out how to design a basic work inventory management system. I presented the concept to my director who was intrigued by my idea. If this could work then we had a chance to get ourselves organized quickly and we could avoid the years' long wait for the IT division to create a custom solution for us. If my idea didn't work, no harm done, but we'd still be in the same pickle with mounting overtime and brokers who were starting to take their business to our competitors.

After some development, testing, and training, the department had a new inventory management system that allowed them to catch up on overtime within a couple of weeks. They eventually were able to process new clients and renewals at a much quicker pace, making them the fastest in the industry, and well ahead of the competition. This project moved quickly because I was able to work independently with my idea and take a heads down focus once I knew what had to be done.

I am proud of this project. I had a good time being curious, creative and learning a new way to deal with an old problem. I was also thrilled to help the department reduce day-to-day stresses, improve efficiencies, move to number one in the industry, and create a better workplace for all.

This project worked well with a one-person team, and yes, I was able to move quickly to a solution. But I missed out on the shared experience of a team effort, the honeymoon phase of a new team, and the final celebratory feeling of a job well done. Let's just say the wrap-up party was light on the wings and beer.

Over time, I could see how much fun it was to do things with others, not to mention how much better the process and end result often is.

LEARNING ABOUT ME

Biologically, we're wired to focus on what's wrong with us. I see this all the time in my work. When my clients move through a problem or towards a goal, they're often analyzing what's wrong with them and what's wrong with others – always what's wrong.

It takes me a while to get them to see the positive side and what's working. It's so much easier to have a critical lens.

The move from Me to We doesn't happen quickly. We must first become self-aware. *Know thyself,* they say. But how do we do that?

One of the tools I used was a personality assessment tool called the Type Coach Verifier Plus – an assessment tool that helps you determine your personality preferences and style, and where you are on any of the four personality dimension scales: Extrovert/Introvert; Sensor/Intuitive; Thinker/Feeler; and Judger/Perceiver.

I was not surprised when I learned that my personality type preference is the most independent of the 16 types. It turns out I also have a rare type. The INTJ woman – Introvert, Intuitive, Thinker, Judger – is uncommon with only 0.5% of us out there. I've never met another INTJ woman, so I suppose this is true.

Like many others, my first thought was to see elements of my personality style that I felt were less than attractive. When I see phrases like *can be intense, should smile more and frown less, is often uncomfortable giving compliments,* or *can be direct to the point of being blunt,* I wince. Like most of us, I hyper-focused on these areas. Along the way, I learned how to focus more on the positives: *capacity to work for LONG stretches, incredible will power* (except when it comes to chocolate), *constant pursuit for the best in themselves, drive to reach closure, strategic visionary, confident, have solutions pop into their head out of nowhere,* or *catch on to a new idea or concept quickly.*

As I learned more about the different type preferences, I grew to appreciate the nuances of my preferred style and why I sometimes behave the way I do. Digging deeper, I learned more about the other 15 types as well and developed an appreciation for the style of others. We all have our own ways of looking at things – the direction we naturally lean toward, different triggers, different viewpoints, and how we respond to stress.

As I learned more about myself, I could see that my approach made sense to me, but not always to others, and vice versa. I was learning that we all wear a different set of glasses and we view the world through a different lens.

Another tool I used to gain more self-awareness was the *Values in Action Character Strengths* survey which focuses on character strengths. We all possess the 24 strengths, but as I found out, we each express them in different ways. Some character strengths we use more than others and some, such as Bravery, we use only when the need arises.

When my clients go through an assessment to find out their top character strengths, one of the first things they do is jump to the bottom of the list looking for what they perceive as their weaknesses. "I need to work on Self-Regulation," they say, as they see it last on their list. But then I tell them that Self-Regulation is the lowest strength worldwide and perhaps that makes them feel a little better.

In getting to know ourselves, finding out our top strengths is key. We learn what's inherently awesome about us, how we naturally show up in the world, and what is most energizing to us.

Diving deeper into my strengths, I soon discovered that my love of reading, watching documentaries, and taking courses was an expression of my top strength: Love of Learning. My endless questions as both a child and as an adult, and my willingness to try almost anything new, just once, are an expression of another top strength: Curiosity.

Although I'm not practiced at art or creative writing, I express my strength of Creativity in the problem-solving realm. It's fun to think of five more ways to do something. "It's never impossible

– there's always a way," is a favourite saying of mine. I never knew this is how I expressed my signature strength of Creativity, because for me, the creative fun is in the discovery.

Learning these things about myself, and about the whole range of character strengths, enabled me to see people from a different viewpoint. I no longer expected them to be just like me. I learned to see the whole bouquet of strengths and to appreciate what is best about others.

Learning more about myself and accepting myself (warts and all) were the first steps in making my shift from Me to We. I had to be courageous enough to be vulnerable and to be okay with who I was – to recognize the beautiful parts and to be accepting of the not so beautiful. When I was able to do this, I started seeing the world through a different lens.

The shift to trusting and letting people in was no easy task. My *a-ha* moment came when I learned to open up to others about my life and ask for help. I had struggled for years with the effects of living with loved ones who suffered from serious mental illness and alcoholism. Being independent and very private were two of my many survival skills.

LEARNING ABOUT WE

Belgian Draft horses are known for being incredibly strong. Their main use is as farm horses, and they're *huge*. A full-grown horse might be as tall as six or seven feet at the shoulder. On their own, a full-grown horse weighing 2,000 lbs. can pull four times its own weight, or 8,000 lbs. But when they work together, they can do remarkable things.

The more I fully embraced and became aware of my personality preferences and character strengths, the more I began to see others in a different light. I learned how to spot strengths in people I interacted with on a regular basis. I began to appreciate others' attention to detail and requests for evidence, their preference for advanced planning or the last-minute, fly-by-the-seat-of-your-pants approach, the leadership style with a touch of humor and buckets of kindness, or the relationship-first approach versus my focus on logic.

I particularly appreciate seeing others display character strengths that are not among the highest for me. For example, I enjoy seeing Humor used when someone lightens the mood at just the right moment, or sees things from a different angle and delivers that view with dry wit. I'm fascinated when witnessing someone high in Bravery who continuously stands up for their beliefs and values even in the face of opposition and ridicule. I personally know four such women and I'm in awe of their courage and conviction. I'm also a fan of those individuals high in Social Intelligence who seem to always know just the right thing to say or, perhaps more importantly, the right thing not to say.

Admittedly, I'm still hesitant to be fully immersed in groups. I prefer the *on the edge* consultant role, with a high element of autonomy. I like to move quickly but still have high quality work, pivot where it makes sense, and stay away from project politics. But being part of a group means I get to exercise my patience and tolerance. I also like to complete what I start and know that not everyone has the strength of Perseverance to do this. Others are able to move on to the next project and dislike the post-mortem, clean-up, and closure part, but I feel it's necessary. It allows me to get feedback, measure results, and know what worked well and what didn't so we can avoid repeating the same mistakes. As I like to say, "Bless the world, bless yourself, finish well," and working in teams means I have to give up control over these things which often translates into more stress for me. There was a time when I chose to avoid this extra stress but now I look for opportunities to work with others on projects that have big potential. I can see the light at the end of the tunnel as teams move through the stages of forming, storming, and norming to eventually performing. I'm excited about what we can do together and I know that moving through the stressful times is worth it. I enjoy the amazing results that we create together and especially the relationships that we develop along the way. Not to mention the celebrations.

I now see how everyone around me brings something amazing to the table. Each of us, when supported and cheered, brings gifts and talents that make the whole team so much better. When other's strengths are different than mine, we can complement each other – they can fill the gaps and holes, and make things stronger.

A single Belgian Draft horse, at 2,000 lbs, can pull an unthinkable 8,000 lbs. But when trained together with another farm horse, a teammate, they can pull a jaw-dropping 32,000 lbs. The We is indeed mightier than the Me.

ABOUT THE AUTHOR
SUSAN KUZ

Susan Kuz is a positive psychology practitioner. She designs programs and courses that help organizations improve employee and team effectiveness, health, and well-being.

She holds a Bachelor of Commerce (hons) with the Asper School of Business at the University of Manitoba, a Certificate in Applied Positive Psychology with the Flourishing Centre in NYC, is certified as an Applied Positive Psychology Coach, a certificated facilitator of The Passion Test; Type-Coach Communication Systems; Flourishing Skills Groups; Appreciation Languages in the Workplace, and a graduate of Mindfulness-Based Strengths Practice program from the VIA Character Institute. She also instructs at the University of Winnipeg's Professional Applied and Continuing Education programs on topics related to positive organizations and leadership.

Susan is passionate about learning the newest and best tools for cultivating positive personal growth and navigating through change. To access the Type-Coach and VIA tools referenced in Susan's chapter go to: www.susankuz.com/courage-to-change-resources/

Contact:
susan@susankuz.com
(204) 801-4389
www.SusanKuz.com

9 | EATING ELEPHANTS
by Kim Hruba

When people ask me about the exact timing of the when and how and I knew I wanted to be a writer, I cringe.

I don't like to disappoint people, so before I know what's happening, my Minnesota Nice kicks in and I'm diving headfirst into my childhood, frantically searching for a reason that explains my transformation from a regular person to a creative one.

Maybe it was all the freedom I had growing up. My grandparents owned a lake resort and all of us cousins on my mom's side lived there. We kids had free rein to swim whenever we wanted and to explore wherever we wanted. This included venturing past two other resorts, through a small wood, and down another road a quarter mile to buy candy cigarettes at The Snuggle Inn.

Or maybe I should credit my grandmother. She was an elementary school teacher and artist. Oil paints and watercolors were her main medium, but she also dabbled in acting, poetry, and macramé before settling on stained glass as her primary art form in her later years. She also brought her creativity to the kitchen where I would watch her concoct culinary creations like Seven Bean Salad with improvised ingredients such as peanut butter or chocolate cake with beer.

I journaled as a child – something I learned only recently

most kids don't do.

But, other than getting hearings aids in the 6th grade, I would argue that my childhood was pretty normal. Every summer I fell in the lake and got at least one badly scraped knee riding my bike. During the school year, fear of missing the bus always propelled me from my warm bed and out to the bus stop in the nick of time.

I was not poring over Jane Austen at age 8 or unwittingly scribbling out masterpiece poems by age 10. I was embarrassingly boy crazy and that is pretty much all I wrote about in my girl diaries. *Did he like me? Did he not? Did I like him back?* Unrequited love, although something with which I was extensively familiar, was not a phrase I would learn until Kate Winslet used it in *The Holiday* when I was already 31, not 13.

And, like all children, I grew up.

Eventually, I figured out when people asked me about the details of how I became a writer, what they really wanted to hear was that I was a child prodigy. That I was gifted with an innate understanding of metaphor and a knack for alliteration. They wanted me to affirm a belief that I was different. That I was not like them and, therefore, they were not like me. That I was destined to be *une artiste* (with all the flair of the *Fancy Nancy* book series, *ooh la la...*) – and they were not.

Unless you were conceived in a petri dish, I'm here to tell you that the very nature of the fact that you were created by a mother and father is evidence that you were meant to create. Julia Cameron asserts in her book, *The Artist's Way,* that "we are, ourselves, creations. And we, in turn, are meant to continue creativity by being creative ourselves."

In *Big Magic: Creative Living Beyond Fear,* author Elizabeth Gilbert takes this assertion a step further, suggesting that ideas are their own energy form of being. She calls the fairy dust around creation "big magic" – the mystery, the divine juju, or whatever you want to call it – that compels a person to desire creation even if he or she can't draw. That is to say, even if you *were* conceived in a petri dish, as long as you are a living, breathing human being you have the capacity to create. The bar of expectation has already been set low for you. The *universe* has set the bar low for you. All you have to do is have courage to be you and just show up.

COURAGE

Whenever someone tells me he or she can't be an artist, the most common reason cited is an inability to draw. Yes, drawing is art, but it is not the only art. Art is much broader than that. Art is simply creating. Or if "creating" is too fancy a word, all it means is making stuff. Something out of nothing, and – *voila!* And therein lays both the magic and sheer terror of art.

But art is child's play, *non?*

Precisely. Children are filled with copious amounts of self-confidence and curiosity. They aren't concerned about the next book deal or whether they'll get into a prestigious art show or have enough widgets made for the next craft fair. Children create because they enjoy it.

Artists get a bad rap for being expert procrastinators and excuse-makers, but I say the bogeyman is real. That pesky creature of the night that lurks under the bed, in the shadows, in your own brain, is the spook that chokes a body every time. It takes courage to face your fears; to swallow down the disappointment of well-intentioned loved ones from your artistic past. It takes courage to let go of others' expectations as well as your own. It takes courage to create. I like what Kate Winslet's *Holiday* neighbor Arthur calls it: Gumption.

So, how do you do it?

First, start by saying yes to being a creative person. Agree to agree that each person in the universe is a creation and by his or her own birthright is called to create. Even you.

If you feel the need for permission to create, I hereby wave my wand, sprinkle my share of fairy dust, and bless you as a creative being.

BE YOU

There's a lot of romance associated with creating. For one, you have to be "in the mood" or "feel like doing it." The notion of suffering attached to being an artist – poor, starving, aloof, directionless – suggests that artists get a free pass from the responsibilities of the mundane like going to work, paying bills, and doing laundry. Maybe the starving artist of your fantasies wears a beret and sits on a terrace in Paris swirling *un café au lait,* musing over a leather-bound notebook, pages smoky with charcoal shadings. As a mother of five children, my fantasy is travelling and writing cross-country Kerouac style in my minivan. *Alone.* Who thinks about songwriting soccer moms or poetic plumbers? No stereotype or fantasy – no matter how enticing that Parisian coffee or solo road trip might be – does justice to anyone.

I see messy thinkers trying to organize their creativity with lists and timelines and organizers trying to let go of the Microsoft Excel to open themselves up to that elusive stuff called muse. The truth is you can only be yourself. Yes, experiment with different strategies for creating, but stay true to your nature. In *Strengths Finder 2.0,* Tom Rath suggests playing to your strengths instead of trying to develop your weaknesses. That isn't intended to be an argument for letting weaknesses go unchecked, but rather a call to cultivate the assets or things that you're already good at as enjoyable and inspiring in themselves.

Okay, you're probably not going to be banging out Picassos and Rembrandts, so what? Sometimes you have to keep score of the little things to see the big picture. Keep track of all the little ways in which you throw a little creativity into your day and give yourself credit for the ways in which you are (already) creative. Small wins make big gains.

Can't think of anything? Maybe it was in that Sunday dinner you prepared. A particular sentence you crafted in an email. The way you combined home décor elements to make your house feel welcoming. The modifications you made to improve suction on your vacuum. That gizmo you built in the garage. (I don't know much about gizmos in the garage but maybe you do!) The little whiskers you painted on a child's face to complete her black cat Halloween costume. The way you paired your scarf with your ensemble or the tie you selected this morning to complement your mood or to match the crazy socks under that serious suit. A spreadsheet that is absolutely masterful in its capacity to capture and explain data or your PowerPoint presentation that inspired a team. And my favorite creative thing (after chocolate): putting a smile on a person's face with a good joke, a kind word, or a surprise.

The important thing is to be you – *do you* – and find that flash of creativity in all of the things you already do.

JUST SHOW UP

I often compare creating to an exercise program. I'm an expert at exercise programs. I start by aiming high: I'm going to exercise every day for 60 minutes! This soon turns into a pledge to exercise every day for 30 minutes, then every other day plus weekends, then minus weekends. One month later, the exercise program is another relic on the scrap heap of good intentions. The problem is starting out doing too much, too fast, too soon.

Art is the same.

I complained of this to a fellow writer once and she encouraged me to keep lowering the bar until I found a writing regime that worked for my life. So I kept lowering the bar and guess where it landed? Ten minutes. The best program I could stick to was scheduling *ten minutes* for my creative writing.

Ten minutes accommodates the busy-ness of my life. I may not have an hour, or even thirty minutes, but if I have ten minutes to check my Facebook news feed, I have ten minutes to spend on creating. I remind myself that I may not have one 60-minute unit, but I'm pretty sure that I can find six 10-minute units throughout the day.

Ten minutes is just enough time to face the fear of starting. The clock's ticking and the pressure's on to bang out a few lines. There's no time for perfection; only for getting something on the page. Once the timer rings, I have a choice: I can either move on to another task or I can continue. Either way, I get to claim a small victory because I showed up to do *something*.

Sometimes it *is* hard to sit down and create. Less desirable tasks on my to-do list, such as dusting or balancing my checkbook, suddenly become far more appealing when I'm creatively stuck. Ten minutes is long enough to identify the discomfort, breathe, then give space to the brainstorming or tinkering that gets me through that creative bottleneck. This might look like sitting at my desk and only thinking about the thing I want to create. Reading counts too, with bonus points if it's relevant to my project.

Ten minutes has become the sweet spot of my success. There's even a name for this type of time management: the Pomodoro Technique.

When I'm in really good shape, I practice what I call the 3 P's: Process, Practice, Project. Just like an athlete, I start with warm-ups. I journal for ten minutes (Process), then take a writing prompt and write for ten minutes (Practice). Then I start the project I'm working on. Sometimes that's my own creative work, but I also give credit to the creative writing I do for others through my business. Even if it's something as seemingly lackluster as catalog copy or a company newsletter, I commit myself to showing up because the essence of the task – the magic – is still that of creating something out of nothing.

I would like to tell you that I stick to this routine, but honestly, I'm pretty willy-nilly. I adjust to the ebb and flow of a busy life like anyone else. There are days when I *don't* journal. There are days when I journal but skip the writing practice. There are days when I pass on my manuscript, giving priority to clients' projects. But every day I *do* commit to being present in some creative way, even if all that means is giving credit for my storytelling flair at bedtime.

Like a good exercise plan, start slow and low. Sit in the chair for ten minutes. Hold the pen. Maybe drag it across the page and see what happens. Or start writing, fast and furiously, before your mind can catch up and question what you're doing. Jab a thumb into a clump of clay and note how it feels. Get on the floor and build your own LEGO tower. You have a mouth, sing. You have hands, clap. Rearrange your potted plants.

The biggest surprise I've encountered on my creative journey is that, at some point – after the inspiration has been grabbed and the fairy dust has settled – art is work. In the writing world, I have seen many writers know the beginning of a story – and are pretty sure they have a good sense for the ending – but get bogged down by what author Jim Butcher calls "the great swampy middle." This is normal. Compare it to planning a party. Initially you feel jazzed about organizing a fun get-together. You'll invite people, the people will come, and they will leave having had a great time.

But what about a theme for the party? Do you need decorations? Costumes? Who should come? Who *shouldn't* come? Should you book Sparkles the Clown or rent a karaoke machine? Should you *buy* a karaoke machine? Cook or cater? And, *please,* remember the napkins and an extra stash of plastic forks because there are always enough knives.

Life is filled with so many details, that the getting from Point A to Point B is a road travelled for *any* project.

When I get stuck in the unglamorous, swampy middle I have two mental images I go to. First, I remind myself, "How do you eat an elephant?" One bite at a time. Next, I let myself look up at the mountain looming large in my mind's eye. I think about that elephant, lower my head, and train my eyes on my feet. I know that all I need in this moment is to keep my feet moving. I don't even have to be fast. Just one foot in front of the other will eventually get me to the top of that mountain.

Poet Jack Gilbert asks us, "Do you have the courage? Do you have the courage to bring forth this work? The treasures that are hidden inside you are hoping you will say yes."

Don't worry about outcomes. Until you have something, you have nothing. Instead, keep your eyes on your feet and eat that elephant one bite at a time.

ABOUT THE AUTHOR
KIM HRUBA

Kim Hruba is an editor, writing coach, and author with 10 years of experience providing writing services and developmental editing for a variety of projects including manuscripts, speeches, company websites, promotional materials, community newsletters, and visitor guides.

She has a Bachelor's degree in Linguistics from the University of Minnesota and TEFL certificate from Hamline University. She taught English to business leaders and managers at a Berlitz School of Languages in the Czech Republic, before settling in Minnesota, USA, where she founded the Girls Lead leadership program and her business, Red Shoes Writing Solutions.

Her speaking topics include: So You Want to Write a Book, Your Voice Matters, and A Whale Is Not a Shark: How to Transform a Speech into the Written Word. Kim is the reigning Toastmasters District 64 Tall Tales champion.

She is working on her second novel and is the Saturday contributor to the *Wannaskan Almanac,* a daily blog where she shares stories about her family that are (mostly) true.

Contact:
kim@redshoeswriting.com
(218) 469-0204
www.KimHruba.com

ABOUT KEYSTONE SPEAKERS

Based in Winnipeg, Canada, Keystone Speakers started in 2015 when a group of experts in their respective fields decided to create a speakers bureau that would provide a supportive, hands-on community for the ongoing development of speaking and business skills.

Our membership includes speakers from Canada, Australia, and the United States, with collective speaking and training experience in ten countries on five continents. We deliver workshops, keynote speeches, seminars, consulting, coaching, and entertainment. Speaking topics include leadership, process improvement, business growth, personal development, communication, and even magic. The *Cornerstones and Keystones* anthology offers a sampling of the wide-ranging expertise of our membership.

To learn more about Keystone Speakers and the incredible speaking and consulting talent we provide, please visit www.keystonespeakers.ca.

For any inquiry regarding the *Cornerstones & Keystones* book series, or to order additional copies of this book, please email keystonespeakers@gmail.com.